The chitta (mind),
like fire without fuel,
calms down when objects
disappear.

APHORISM No. 68

FIRE
WITHOUT
FUEL

The Aphorisms of Baba Hari Dass

SRI RAMA PUBLISHING
Santa Cruz, California

❖

Edited by Ma Renu & Anand Dass Tabachnick
Design/production by Josh Gitomer & Ann Kelley
Typesetting by Karuna Ault
First Printing, December, 1986
ISBN 0-918100-08-9
Library of Congress Catalog Card No. 86-60051

❖

Other books by Baba Hari Dass:
Silence Speaks
Ashtanga Yoga Primer
A Child's Garden of Yoga
Mystic Monkey
Hariakhan Baba: Known, Unknown
Magic Gem—A Story/Coloring Book
Cat & Sparrow
Sweeper to Saint
The Yellow Book (out of print)

❖

Tapes by students of Baba Hari Dass:
Tender Mercies (Women's Choir)
Horizons—Improvisations for Harp and Flute
Sri Ram Kirtan—Volumes I and II
Jai Ma Kirtan—Songs to the Divine Mother
Guru Purnima Songs

❖

Write for a free catalog of books and tapes.

TABLE *of* CONTENTS

The
PHOTOGRAPHS

These 47 illustrations create
a sketch of Baba Hari Dass' first
15 years in the West.
Seen from the eyes of students,
friends, and acquaintances, these images
reveal a brief cross-section
of the many activities and interests
that fill Babaji's days.

INTRODUCTION

IT IS INTERESTING that this book came about almost by "accident." Someone gave Baba Hari Dass an attractive blank book with a brocade cover and he started filling it. When he had a few spare moments, he would write a page or two just as ideas presented themselves to him. Thus it grew, with no particular order, over a year's time. *Fire Without Fuel,* with minimal editing and organization into chapters, is the result—a collection of aphorisms plus commentary.

Baba Hari Dass has not spoken for the past 34 years; to communicate he writes on a small chalkboard. The teachings and advice that appear on his chalkboard are often much like aphorisms, the nature of which is to offer a profound statement in as few words as possible.

In India, for several thousand years, great philosophical teachings have been passed from *guru* (teacher) to disciple by way of aphorisms, or *sutras* (lit., "threads"), for various reasons. First, a succinct statement can have a profound impact on a student's mind; its terseness makes it memorable and provides the student with a viable seed to meditate upon and eventually bring to full flower. Because such teachings were meant only for the ears of serious seekers—the initiates of a particular school of thought—these obscure "threads" protected esoteric knowledge from the curiosity of the uninitiated. Also, before literacy became widespread, easily memorized aphorisms were a means of preserving knowledge from one generation to another.

Aphorisms are the "keys" to a larger teaching which includes personal instruction and detailed commentary. Without commentary an aphorism is often obscure, even incomprehensible. For example we find the aphorism, "Purified mind is the healer of the body, of birth and of death." Although we are well aware of phychosomatic diseases, we wonder how any state of mind can "cure" birth and death. In lieu of the physical presence of the teacher, we have to study the commentary to discover the *sutra*'s meaning.

The philosophical content of these aphorisms is Babaji's own blend of Samkhya-yoga, Vedantism, and the practical common sense for which he is well-known by his students and readers of his earlier books. Using unpretentious language and simple parables, Babaji takes up the great themes with which philosophy and religion have wrestled throughout the ages. He unhesitatingly informs us that each is responsible for his or her own destiny: "One who waits for God to come remains waiting." If we wish to attain God, or Truth, we must start at once to purify the mind by austerity—that is, by putting limits on our desires. At times he is tough: "The mind doesn't want any discipline; it always makes excuses to avoid it." But under his words there is a deep compassion—he just wants us to be free. He tells us over and over again that we put ourselves in bondage by ignorantly identifying ourselves with the body-mind complex and that "We are always liberated if we only know what bondage is."

Although Baba Hari Dass has been a renunciate for most of his life, having entered an ashram (school or center for monks) at the age of eight, he communicates easily with anyone. Understanding that most of us have to earn our livelihood, that we are often engaged in marriage or other intimate relationship, he is committed to guiding us, without judging, through the traps and delusions of the world: "Be in the world, but not of it." He doesn't expect us to follow his path of renunciation unless there is a strong conviction and a natural tendency in that direction. Indeed, he says that it is often easier for householders to attain liberation because they can support each other in their spiritual aims.

He wants us, above all, to live with peaceful minds. Thus he wrote these pages to show that each one of us, regardless of circumstances, can awaken to the realization that he or she is a reflection of God. —*Ma Renu, Editor*

Chapter I
GOD &
CREATION

1

The world is a mirror in which God's image reflects.

NO ONE CAN DEFINE GOD. If God can be defined by words, then God can't be limitless, omnipresent, omnipotent, and omniscient. But we have to understand that Supreme Power some way, so we use three words that give us some glimpse of God's nature. The words are *sat*, or absolute existence, *chitta**, or absolute consciousness, and *ananda*, absolute bliss.

Every thing that is created or that exists in this universe is a combination of these three energies. When these energies are in their manifest, active forms, they are called *jnana*, consciousness, *ichha*, will to create, and *kriya*, activity in matter. The same energies are also called *sattva guna*, quality of purity, *rajas guna*, quality of activity, and *tamas guna*, quality of inertia.

When we see the world, we are actually seeing the reflection of God's nature, that is, *sat-chid-ananda†*. But our mind is so confused that instead of paying attention to those energies, we pay attention to the form.

---

* *Chitta* can be thought of as the generalized field of awareness, encompassing intellect, ego, and mind.
† When the three words are written as one, *chitta* becomes *chid.*

2

*God is like a magnet
and the creation is like iron
wheels. The iron wheels
rotate simply by the presence
of the magnet.
Similarly the creation
acts by the presence of God.*

IF SEVERAL IRON WHEELS are arranged on an axis and a magnet is put at the center, then all the wheels start rotating. The magnet is not doing anything—not moving or touching the wheels—but its energy is attracting the iron and causing the rotation. If the magnet is removed from its place, then all the wheels will stop rotating. In the creation those wheels are cosmic mind, ego sense, elements, subtle elements, organs of senses, organs of action, etc., and the magnet is God, or *Atman.* The energy of God activates the creative process in nature. God doesn't create anything, but His presence in nature is the cause of creation. If God is separated from nature, then all activity will stop.

3

I am the One, second to none.

THE ONE, THE ABSOLUTE—a fundamental reality that is eternal and without cause—is God, the Cause of causes. All that which is created has always been within the Absolute. The Absolute manifests in the form of a threefold energy: consciousness, will, and matter. Consciousness is a direct evolute from the Absolute, so it comes first; then the "will to create" manifests from the consciousness; from that will, the energy of matter manifests. Matter possesses the energy of both will and consciousness. Will possesses the energy of consciousness in active form and the energy of matter in potential form. Consciousness possesses both the energies of will and matter in potential form. The Absolute flows in all three energies in the form of spirit.

The human mind is finite and the Absolute is infinite, so the concept of the Absolute can't be explained by the finite mind.

The Absolute is omnipresent, omnipotent, omniscient, all perfect, yet it cannot recreate itself. There can't be two absolutes. So all finite beings, by their effort, reach a state where they dissolve into the infinite and the Absolute. The One remains one without a second.

4

Creation is the product of bliss, and bliss is its sustainer; to bliss it returns.

THE SUPREME REALITY is truth, existence, and bliss all together. The universe is a manifestation of that divine being who is experienced in the form of bliss.

This creation is sustained by that bliss in the form of the three gunas, or three powers: consciousness, action, and matter. These three powers together are none other than the divine being, or bliss.

After completing its function, this gross existence merges into its subtle existence; this reality or truth merges into its subtle truth; and the bliss of this creation merges into the bliss of its creator.

5

Evolution is the cause of involution, and vice versa.

INVOLUTION CANNOT OCCUR without the process of evolution taking place first. Evolution begins when the consciousness *(jnana)* and will *(ichha)* combine and give rise to matter *(kriya)*. The resulting energy produces the sound form of Om and is given the name of *Ishwara* (God).

Two main forces work together in the evolutionary process: Supreme Spirit *(Purusha)* and Supreme Matter *(Prakriti)*.* These forces give rise to universal mind *(mahat)*. Universal mind then becomes the main active force, using matter as material, for evolution of the universe. In this way, the creation evolves into sheaths: causal sheath, subtle sheath, and gross sheath.

When matter wants to return to spirit, the process is reversed. The gross sheath dissolves into the subtle sheath, then the subtle into the causal. But the memory of sheaths remains in the Supreme Spirit. Again, that memory becomes the cause of evolution.

---

* See *Samkhya* theory of evolution.

6

Life force is nothing but the activity of the cosmic mind.

IN THE EVOLUTIONARY PROCESS, the first evolute from *mula prakriti* (primordial nature) is *mahat* (cosmic mind). In *mahat* the three main energies, *jnana* (consciousness), *ichha* (will to create), and *kriya* (activity) are in an unbalanced state. This unbalanced state in cosmic mind is the cause of creation. The act of creation itself is a life force. This creation is not happening by coincidence or chance, nor is it unplanned. There is a perfect plan in the cosmic mind and, according to that plan, everything is being created, preserved, and dissolved.

*Anything that exists
will never be destroyed;
its disappearance
is simply a transformation.*

EVERYTHING IS CREATED by the combination of five elements: earth, water, fire, air, and ether. Each element possesses a life energy which causes movement, expansion, growth, and decay in an object. So anything that exists either grows or decays. This transformation never stops.

Some dirt, for example, changes into a lump, and the lump hardens and becomes a rock. This is a transformation of growth. Again the rock tumbles and breaks; each piece knocks against the others until they weaken and crumble into a powder. This is a transformation of decay. This cycle of transformation repeats continuously. When the life force in one element is mixed with other elements, it produces a form, and its life energy also changes. For example, a seed's life energy is to exist and remain alive. But by mixing it with dirt, water, heat, and air, it starts growing. The life energy of the seed changes to a plant's growing energy.

In an animal, life energy is more apparent. All functions, such as eating, acting, or moving can be seen, so we believe that an animal is alive. But in the case of a seed or rock, we don't see it so readily.

When an animal's physical functions cease, we say the animal is dead. Although we see that the animal is not functioning, we are not aware that the life force of each element which constituted that form is still functioning. So actually there is a transformation of life energy in that animal, and one form is changed into a different form. The dead body will decay and change into the earth element, and the earth element's life energy will still work. Similarly the life energies of water, fire, air, and ether elements will go on changing.

Chapter II
SELF ~ GOD
WITHIN a BEING

8

*God within a being is called
Atman, or Purusha.*

GOD IS NO DIFFERENT FROM THE SELF
which resides in every being. But this secret
is not revealed to the ordinary person whose
mind is not purified. As long as we identify
with the mind—which is limited to time, space, and causation—our consciousness can't develop enough to break
through those limitations.

If someone carries a ten dollar bill in his pocket and
doesn't know about it because it is hidden among some
scraps of paper, then he will never feel that he has ten
dollars. So it is with the Self. Our ego, attachments, and
limitations are veils which cover the *Atman* and make it
seem separate. When these veils are removed, the mind
will lose its separate identity and there will be only
Atman.

9

The Self is beyond birth, death, gender, class, and religion—only the body wears those labels.

THE SELF IS PURE CONSCIOUSNESS—it is beyond the characteristics of the mind. Pleasure, pain, anger, hate, attachment, anxiety are within the mind, and they are expressed by sensory responses in the body.

The mind controls the gross body, which is simply matter, composed of five elements. Nevertheless, this gross body is the mark of a living being. All of the labels worn by this body—such as black, white, Christian, Jew, man, woman—take birth and die.

The Self is omnipresent, omniscient, omnipotent, and beyond all forms. When the Self is trapped within the body, the indicator of the Self, "I," starts identifying with the body. This wrong identification is called ignorance. The real "I" is not the body, mind, or life force *(prana)*. It is pure consciousness and can't wear the same labels worn by the gross body.

10

Souls are numberless—
any number of souls may be
added or subtracted;
still they remain numberless.
The soul is pure consciousness,
yet labeled with qualities.

THE SOUL, OR SELF, within beings cannot be numbered by counting the bodies. The body is a form; it can be numbered. But the soul is formless, a supreme energy by which presence the body functions. A potter makes a pitcher; as soon as the form of the pitcher appears, air is present inside of it. The number of pitchers may increase or decrease, but that doesn't affect the air. In the same way, the soul can't be affected whether the number of beings increases or decreases.

The soul, or the Self, is pure consciousness, immortal, and self-luminous. But, due to ignorance, the soul is seen taking birth, suffering in the world, and dying. All of these characteristics are of the body and mind. The air inside a clay pitcher will take on the odor of that which has been kept in the pitcher. We say, "This pitcher's air smells like sandalwood," or "This pitcher's air smells bad." Although the pitchers are clean and air has no odor of its own, the air inside the pitcher smells. The Self is like that same air, taking on the aroma of an individual's good and bad qualities. The Self itself is neither good nor bad.

11

*The body is the temple
of the soul
and the soul is the temple
of God.*

A BODY CONSISTS OF THE MIND, sense organs, and a physical form that is visible. In that physical form the soul is like a king whose presence makes the mind, senses, and body function. The soul in the body is the supreme authority; and the body is the temple of the soul wherein it dwells.

The individual soul is not independent; within it there is the energy of God. God's reflection is always in the soul, so we can say the soul is a temple of God.

12

*The self and the Supreme Self
are the same but
their purposes are different,
like the ocean and the
water pond.*

THE WATERS OF THE OCEAN and the pond, except for their saline content, are exactly the same, but they are used differently. On the ocean, ships go from one place to another; different kinds of water-animals, big and small, live there and enjoy their freedom. A change of weather doesn't affect its vastness. The water of the pond is used for drinking and irrigation. It is limited in size and can accommodate only small animals or fish.

The Supreme Self is that ocean where all beings find and enjoy their freedom; the individual self is that pond which fills up in the rainy season and dries out in the summer heat.

The three main energies—consciousness, action, and matter—are the same in the Supreme Self and in the individual self, but there is the difference of limitlessness and limitedness.

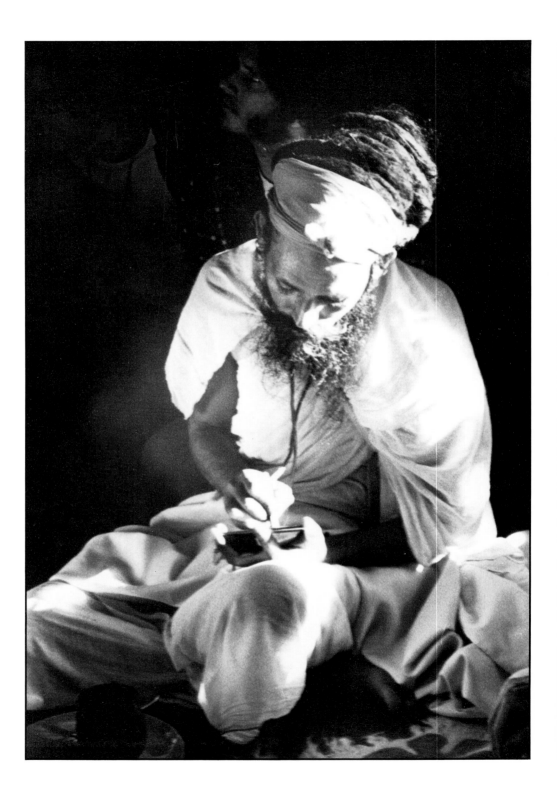

Chapter III
MIND ~ITS FUNCTIONS and ITS FANTASIES

13

*Just as a light is the cause
of projection of a film
on a screen, so the light
of the Self is the cause
of projection of the world
on the mind.*

IN A PERSON there is a film of the world in the form of memory. That memory remains dormant until it is projected on the screen of the mind. Just as a film is projected by light, in the same way the memory is projected by some inner light. What is that light? Some say it's another mind, and some say it's something different than the mind. In both cases we have to admit that the light is coming from a different source. You may call it higher mind, or cosmic mind, the Self, or God.

The film (memory), the light (Self), and the screen (mind) are already present in a newborn child and will remain with that being. They why can't a child relate to the world in the same way as an adult? It is because the projection of the world on the mind appears gradually, just as a film starts at one end and rolls through time.

14

Mind is a mirror in which the light of the soul reflects.

THE MIND IS INVISIBLE. It is recognized only by actions and reactions which are seen in the body and thoughts. Primarily, it is thought, continuously appearing and disappearing, to which we give the name "mind". We can say that mind is an instrument of consciousness; we can say that it is a storehouse of memories. Actually, it is like a mirror in which past actions recur and can be seen as images of the present.

Our past starts with the time an individual soul first came into existence. At that time there were only two things: the soul, or *atman*, and the mind, or *buddhi*. But gradually actions and reactions in the mind created *samskaras*.* Those *samskaras* started reflecting in that mirror of mind and covered the reflection of the soul, which in the beginning was the first and only reflection. But *samskaras* do not wipe out the reflection of the soul; it is always there, activating the mind.

When those *samskaras* of the mind, which appear in the form of thoughts, desires, and memories are removed by the practice of Yoga, then the mirror is perfectly clean and there remains only the one reflection of *atman*. So long as that mirror exists, the reflection of *atman* is there, and when that mirror is finally broken, the *atman* is absorbed into *Paramatman* (the Supreme Soul).

---

* Impressions; conditioning.

15

*Finding right soil,
a seed germinates;
finding mind, senses, and
objects, samskaras germinate.*

SAMSKARAS ARE PRINTS of actions in the mind which are like seeds. Sometimes the term *karma* is used to mean *samskaras*.

Samskaras are identified as thoughts, desires, and tendencies in the mind which lead to action and re-action. Just as a seed remains dormant without the right soil and weather conditions, the *samskaras* also remain dormant as long as they do not contact the mind, senses, and objects. For example, a person in coma will not desire anything because the mind has ceased to identify any object. The *samskara* of desiring is dormant, but if the person comes out of the coma, the same seed will become potent.

Another example we can take: A person goes to a gambling hall with his friend with no intention of gambling—he doesn't even know where he is going. His friend starts gambling and wins. Now. this person's desire to gamble starts growing. He borrows money from his friend and starts gambling. Here the object, which was the gambling situation, created a desire in the mind to gamble. If that person had not gone into the hall, that desire would have remained dormant.

Sometimes people say, "How is it that everyone in an airplane accident gets killed at the same time? Do they have similar *samskaras?*" We all have some common *samskaras* and some particular *samskaras*. Common *samskaras* are like those of taking birth, growing to maturity, getting old, and dying. Particular *samskaras* are illustrated when one brother becomes a thief, while a second brother becomes a scholar. In an airplane accident all the passengers have one common *samskara* of death, which until then has remained dormant. The airplane becomes the right soil for that seed of *samskara* to ger-

minate. The airplane flies up and drops down due to some mechanical failure, and everyone gets killed at the same time.

We don't have control over *samskaras* that appear as fate or destiny, but we can control our thoughts and desires in the present so as to make good *samskaras* for the future.

16

*Evolution and involution
are both expansion
of the mind. One expands
illusion and creates the world,
and the other
expands consciousness
and reveals the truth .*

OSMIC MIND *(MAHAT)* is the cause of all
creation. In the cosmic mind, consciousness,
energy, and matter start working together and
give birth to the subtle elements, the gross
elements, the energy of the senses, etc., and in that way
the whole universe is created. It's just the cosmic mind
that is expanding from its subtlest state to its grossest
state, and we call it evolution. But we don't see the gross
creation as a cosmic mind; it appears real, which is an
illusion created by the ego mind. The more the mind
goes toward its grosser forms, the more illusion it creates.
For example, iron is a metal in the illusory world, but in
reality it's an energy of the cosmic mind. Now the iron
appears in the form of a knife, hammer, car, ship, etc; all
these are separate illusions and they can be numberless.

In involution the process is reversed. The mind, which
had been seeing the reality of the illusion, starts seeing
the reality of cosmic mind in all objects. The mind is expanding toward its subtlest form, which is omniscience,
omnipotence, and omnipresence, or Truth, Reality, God
without limit.

17

While consciousness is a language of the Self, thinking, feeling, and acting are the language of the mind.

ACCORDING TO YOGA, there are four aspects of mind: *manas* (recording faculty), *buddhi* (discriminating faculty), *ahamkar* (identifying faculty), and *chitta* (overall mind which keeps a record of all actions and gives the final judgment). The nature of the mind is to think and feel and to direct the senses to act accordingly. We use this activity of the mind like a language to express ourselves in the world.

When the mind turns inward and purifies itself by meditation, it forgets its language of thinking and feeling. There ensues a state of mind called *samadhi*. The mind of four aspects no longer exists and there remains only the Supreme Power that is guiding the mind, the Self. The Self is actionless, but still there are actions. Those actions are created by the language of the Self, called higher consciousness or *viveka jnana*.

18

*A person
knows what he knows.
An animal knows, but
doesn't know what he knows.*

IN A HUMAN BEING AND AN ANIMAL there is the difference of self-consciousness. A person and an animal both eat, sleep, feel cold, heat, and pain; but the animal doesn't know that it individually knows pain, hunger, or fatigue. A human, however, says, "I am hungry," "I am cold," "I want this," and so on. A human and an animal will both try to achieve physical comfort: if it rains, both will run to stand under a tree for protection. A person is capable of individualizing his/her consciousness and can imagine the cause and effect of any change or action. An animal can feel, but can't individualize its consciousness because it has no "I" sense.

One is aware of one's appearance because there is an individual consciousness that makes one see oneself different from others. A dog, however, doesn't know if it is a pretty dog or an ugly dog. It will know that it is not a cat; its instincts will indicate that the cat is of a different family. It will also be able to tell the difference between other species of dogs, as they differ by shape size, and behavior.

Because of this knowledge of "I" consciousness, a human being is superior to all other beings. Without "I" consciousness one can't realize the cause and effects of pain, pleasure, attachment, repulsion, and the like, so one can't try to get out of these obstructions. Animals take birth with a collective instinctual knowledge and live in the world with all its sufferings. Without knowing the cause, they die without ever trying to get out of suffering.

"I" consciousness is the first awakening in humans: "I am a person," (not an animal). Then the same "I" consciousness individualizes the person in all his actions,

thoughts, behavior, stature, and the person completely accepts that he or she is that particular body and mind. Due to that same "I" consciousness, the knowledge of the Self as the main cause of creation is completely forgotten and that person remains rotating in the cycle of birth, growth, decay, and death—just like an animal. In Yoga, "I" consciousness is called *asmita klesha*. It is classified as an affliction and a hindrance to attaining higher consciousness.

There is always a chance for a person to break out of that cycle, but there is no such chance for an animal unless it incarnates as a human and develops "I" consciousness.

19

Our inhalations and exhalations are thinking and acting processes that control life.

A PERSON INHALES AND EXHALES 21,600 times in twenty-four hours. Within that twenty-four hours the mind thinks and acts through the body or in dreams.

When we inhale the air goes in and divides into five pranic energies which feed different parts of the body, including the mind. At the same time, the mind thinks. When we exhale, the breath acts through the body and, for a while, the thinking process stops.

In *pranayama* (breath control) the exhaling process consumes twice the time as the inhaling process. It creates a stage of nothingness. In martial arts the action is done with an exhalation because the body, already strengthened by the inhalation, needs to act.

In this way inhalation and exhalation complete two parts of life, that is, thinking and acting. They also create life force *(prana)*, which activates the whole body mechanism.

20

Intelligence is only proper use of the senses.

SOME ARE BORN with the quality of being able to use the senses properly, and some develop that quality when they grow up.

The senses are hearing, feeling, seeing, tasting, smelling. These senses don't work independently; there is a mind behind the senses.

Proper use of the senses means the mind is attentive when one or more of the senses is functioning. For example, there is a teacup on the table; the sense of seeing will see it. If the mind is not attentive, then the mind will not notice if there is tea in the cup or not. If the mind is attentive, the eye will see the cup, the nose will smell the tea, the feeling of its heat will be recognized when touched, and the mind will gather complete knowledge of the object.

The mind's function is to receive from and give to the senses. The senses are instruments that collect information from the outside world and give it to the mind; the mind then passes this information to the higher mind for examination and discrimination. It relates to the information with its individuality (ego) and gives the final judgment. The whole process happens very quickly and the senses will act toward the object according to the final judgment.

The senses are closer to us than the mind because we use them all the time, knowingly or unknowingly. We can't imagine a thing very easily by simply using the mind. But if a thing is perceived by the senses, it doesn't take much time to bring its memory back in the mind. If the object is perceived correctly through the senses, then it will create a correct memory of the object. In this way, correct knowledge will be collected, and that will develop intelligence.

For example: A rope is perceived as a snake. The information goes to the higher mind to examine, discriminate, and give judgment. The higher mind develops fear of the snake and wrong knowledge is collected.

If the mind is attentive to all our sense perceptions, then all the information gathered will give right knowledge. The right knowledge will reinforce attentiveness of the mind. In this way intelligence is developed. So by simply using the senses properly, one can be intelligent.

21

*A wise person is one who sees
the effect of an action
before he acts.*

OUR MIND IS TRAINED to act immediately without thinking of the outcome. For example, a fly sits on a person's arm; he slaps his arm and the fly is dead. The person did not mean to kill the fly, but the mind was so quick to act that it did not bother to know the consequences of its act. The mind acts in this way ninety percent of the time. It is ignorance when the mind simply acts without seeing its result beforehand. Contrary to this, a wise person's mind is trained to see the consequences before he acts. Like an army general, or a chess player, one sees the effect of every move before one acts.

22

God is the master of nature and we are its servants.

HUMANS ARE THE MOST INTELLIGENT beings in the creation. The cosmic energy is much stronger in us than in all other creatures, so we have more understanding of the creation and how it is controlled. Therefore, we are responsible for protecting this creation from our self-created evils. We are responsible for the care of the lower animals, the earth, water, trees, and mountains. We should see ourselves as servants of this creation.

23

The world within the mind is the cause of the external world; or say, the world is a projection of our own desires.

THE WORLD APPEARS when the mind functions. The world disappears when the mind stops. If one is unconscious, it is plain that the world doesn't exist. But there *is* a world that always exists, whether one is awake, asleep, or unconscious—a physical world like a house or a car. The mind creates a world of its own over that physical world, giving a shape and a color to objects and creating a relationship with them according to its desire.

A church, temple, or mosque is seen as very sacred by devotees; but if enemies invade, they won't see it in the same way. These people won't hesitate to burn or ruin it. A woman is seen differently by her lover than by her brother because their desires are different. In this way, the whole world that is seen and experienced through our senses is a projection of our desires. When our desires change, the object also changes. For example, your intimate friend visits you and you see him as beautiful. Then the friend steals your watch from your table and you get into a fight. Now your desire is changed. The friend changes into your enemy, and his form also changes from beautiful to ugly, in your eyes.

The world as perceived by our senses appears to be true and real as long as the mind is polluted by desires. When the mind is purified and pure consciousness is developed, then the projected world will disappear and there will remain one reality.

24

One can't see someone else's dream; nor can one see another's world.

A DREAM IS MANIFESTED by desires, imagination, and a memory of the past. Each person's world is manifested by desires, attachment, and ego. Just as you can be in someone's dream but can't see you are in it, in the same way one can be a part of someone's world but can't see that person's world.

In someone's dream, a whole story can be built up around you as the main actor in the dream. The dreamer can take you to different places—hiking, fishing, or getting involved in accidents. The dreamer feels pleasure, pain, or fear in the dream, but it doesn't affect you because it is not your dream. In the same way, we make our own worlds. Say that you are building a house and you hire several people to help you build. If the house burns down you feel pain, sadness, and loss. It doesn't affect the other builders the same way because the house is in your world as "yours." For the others, it is just one of many houses.

Our world is our desires, attachments, and the sense of ego which establishes a relationship with objects. That relationship we have created is mixed with attachment, aversion, pleasure, pain, hope, and despair. Relationships, society, possessions—all are parts of our world. We are attached to them and feel a strong bond with them, but it's only a mental creation—just like a dream. In the same way, everyone creates his or her own world in which others are included, but no one sees another's world.

25

*If one had not enjoyed
pleasures and pains as real,
how could there be
an experience of enjoyment?*

PLEASURE IS AN UNDERSTANDING accepted by the mind. When that understanding is rejected by the mind, pain results.

For example, a man marries a woman. He accepts her as his wife. It is simply an understanding, created by his mind, that the woman is his wife. In fact in the body of the woman there is nothing which makes her his wife, but she too feels as his wife. The man gets pleasure due to her friendship. Should his wife divorce him (although there is nothing actually to divorce) he will feel pain because he is forced to relinquish the understanding that the woman is his wife.

One who understands that pleasure and pain are created by the mind enjoys nothing as real and can't retain the memory of pleasure and pain. Due to the lack of that memory, the person's mind can't dwell in the past but remains in the present in every second.

Chapter IV
IGNORANCE & SUFFERING

26

Complete forgetfulness of past identities is death.

PHYSICAL DEATH occurs when the mind ceases to function, the heart ceases to work, the lungs cease to inhale and exhale, and all senses stop their activities. The soul leaves the body, and we say the person is dead. It's not a complete death of the whole person, because the subtle body leaves the physical body in the form of a seed. That seed possesses the prints, *samskaras*, of all the person's actions.

Samskaras are the cause of reincarnation. But in that new birth we completely forget who or where we had been. The whole past is forgotten and the soul appears separate from one lifetime to the next lifetime. This state of forgetfulness is death.

One who remains aware from one life to the next life was never dead.

27

Identification with the body is birth.

WHEN A SOUL INCARNATES in the form of a being, the ego of "I am this body" develops. As long as one doesn't know "I am this body," one has not actually taken birth in the body. It is the birth of ignorance that gives identification with the body.

Enlightened beings are not born because there is no ignorance, and they never die because they don't forget the past. So we say an enlightened being—like Krishna, Buddha, Jesus—is beyond birth and death.

28

Identification with the mind is the cause of all suffering.

"I AM THE MIND"—when this notion is deeply imprinted on the mind, all suffering begins. The mind seeks for pleasure or dwells in pain. Pleasure creates desires; but desires develop dissatisfaction, and this leads to pain. Pain gives birth to fear, fear develops anger, and this leads to separation or ignorance.

The mind is formed by desires, thoughts, ideas, imagination, and memories. In any desire or thought, it is the mind that is the "I" desiring or thinking; "I would like . . . " "I think that . . . " We accept that we are the mind, but the mind has a limited vision; it can't see reality. It sees only its own desires. So the Truth remains unknown and the mind dwells in its own ignorance, which is the cause of all suffering.

29

*Violence
and ego consciousness
can't be separated.
So long as there is individuality
to be defended,
there will be violence.*

EGO CONSCIOUSNESS brings an awareness of "my and mine" in every perception, action, feeling, idea, and object. This "I-ness" is called ego consciousness, for it is a form of ego that creates a relationship with any object. Without this ego consciousness, we cannot adjust to life in the world. It gives us knowledge, such as, "I am cold," "I am hot," "I am unhappy." Anything that comes to the mind, or is created by the mind, is always stamped by the ego: "I did this," "I know it," etc. This ego consciousness separates us and creates individuality. "I am separate from the object outside. The object belongs to me, or doesn't belong to me." All this is the function of ego consciousness.

Because we are separate from others, so we always defend our individuality by our actions, thoughts, and speech. We are like guards who are watching the bank; they are always ready to shoot anyone who tries to loot it. This act of defending individuality is itself an act of violence.

30

*Misery starts
when the mind seeks for
pleasure of the senses.*

WE HAVE TEN SENSES. Five are senses of perception (ears to hear, skin to feel, eyes to see, tongue to taste, nose to smell) and five are senses of action (mouth to talk, hands to grab, feet to walk, genitals to reproduce, and anus to excrete).

The senses of perception are the masters of the senses of action. Upon contact with an object, the senses of perception get attracted to it. This attraction brings desire for the object, and the motor organs strive to obtain it. Desire creates possessiveness, competition, and comparison. Anger comes when the desire is obstructed; pain, when the object is not achieved. Thus delusion is created in the mind, and a person loses the discrimination of what is right and what is wrong.

When a person loses the sense of right and wrong, life becomes miserable. Such a person lives in darkness and forgets the aim, which is to discover the reason for one's existence and how to achieve liberation. One drifts in the vast ocean of the world on the waves of desire, with dreams rising and falling like the tides. One may dream one is a king and owns everything, and again may dream one has lost everything and is a beggar. In reality the ocean remains the same; but the waves and tides of desire create pleasure and pain, illusion and delusion.

So long as the heart is not purified, the senses cannot develop dispassion for the world.

31

Pain and suffering–both
are identified by the mind;
one is physical
pain and one is mental.

WHAT IS PAIN? We all have experienced it. If a person gets hit on his finger, he screams with pain. The blow injures nerves in the skin and creates uncomfortable feelings which are relayed to the mind. The mind identifies those feelings as pain.

Pain is of two kinds: physical pain (injury, fever, abscess, chest pain, etc.) and emotional pain which is felt only in the mind. As an example of the latter: a person blames you for no reason; you feel sad, depressed, and afraid. The mind feels discomfort and you say, "I am suffering from sadness or depression." It means that your mind is bearing pain due to that blame.

Pain and suffering both are identified by the mind. If the mind is unconscious, it feels neither physical nor emotional pain. In some cases, physical pain can cause emotional pain when the mind doesn't accept the pain. That nonacceptance disturbs the mind and an uneasy, distressful state appears in the mind. Emotional pain can also create physical pain, like headache, stomach ache, fever, etc. The reason is that the mind identifies both pains as unaccepted feelings.

Do we have to have suffering? Yes, so long as we are attached to life, to the world, we can't avoid it. Suppose a person lives in a palace where everything is available and he or she can't get injured by any outer means. Will that person be happy? No, there is always a possibility of physical sickness and discontentment due to some unfulfilled desires.

Everyone wants to be happy and to live in peace. Pain, pleasure, desire, and fear come because we don't accept life completely. We take birth, grow up, get old, and die, but we are always trapped by our ideas and expectations.

We desire various things in the world and we expect to live forever to enjoy them. To live immortally was never a reality in the past and it will never be a reality in the future.

Chapter V
HAPPINESS & CONTENTMENT

32

*Life is not a burden;
we make it a burden by not
accepting life as it is.*

WHAT IS LIFE? It is a continuing process of taking birth, growing, decaying, and finally dying. We take birth, we desire things, we get attached to objects. Then we fight for possessions and worry about not having our desires fulfilled. This creates anger, hate, and jealousy. In this way, from birth to death we carry a burden of pain. The cause of the pain is self-created desires and the resulting attachment to desired objects.

Contentment exists when life is accepted as it is. Enjoy what comes to you, don't desire pleasures, don't get attached to the objects of senses, and accept death as a part of life; then you will not carry a burden of pain and you will live in the world peacefully.

A method for achieving peace: first put limits on your desires. Then gradually reduce the limits. That will automatically limit the pains. When the desires are reduced to nothing, the burden of pain will be lifted from your shoulders forever.

33

*The more we accept living
with nature, the
more peace we attain.*

NATURE IS A GIANT MACHINE WHICH creates everything that is needed, such as water, fire, plants, animals, humans. Everything has its own purpose. Even a worm that is destroying a fruit tree is useful in some other area. Everything that is created has its own life span, its purpose, its time, its own speed, its own area (space). If that nature is disturbed somehow, then the individual's nature is also disturbed. For example: a fish that naturally lives in a river is kept in a pond; the change in the nature of the outer environment of the fish will affect its inner nature. Even if the fish is well fed, the freedom of the river will be removed and the peace of the fish will be disturbed.

A human being's life span is up to 100 years. If somehow a person is kept alive for 200 years, will it give peace? If a mountain goat is left in the plains, how would its peace be affected? If a lion is fed grain and a deer is fed meat, how would it affect their natures? How does it affect a person's temperament to always use cars, airplanes, trains, and not to use one's own legs, or to live in a house that is mechanically heated or cooled?

We may not notice the effect of all this change in nature right away, but it always affects our life energy, physical energy, and mental energy. To cure that effect, we use more unnatural means, and that again affects us in some different and negative ways.

Is it possible to prevent all disease, wars, and natural disasters in an effort to achieve universal peace? The answer is no. Nature can't function without its negative force. Destruction always goes with production; neither destruction nor production can exist alone. Night and day, winter and summer, destruction and production are complementary.

The more we change nature, the more it gets polluted. By changing it, we can't make it better, because man has no power to make nature better than it already is. So many toxic gases are in the air due to the burning of petroleum in cars, engines, factories; the water is polluted because so many poisonous substances are manufactured by human beings and dumped in the earth or in bodies of water. Increased population is overcrowding space. Loss of jungles, animals, and even worms is affecting na-

ture's natural process of purifying itself. In this way, the more we remove ourselves from nature, the more pain we create.

Nature has its own process of creation, preservation, and destruction. If this process is accepted as it is, only then can peace be attained.

34

*Happiness is attained
when the inner and outer
states of the mind
are in harmony.*

THE MIND HAS BOTH AN INNER AND AN outer way of expressing itself. In its inner state it is always discontented and creating desires, while in its outer state it is always looking for quick gratification. The result is discontentment, anger, fear, and jealousy.

It is not possible for a person to simply stop all desires and stop seeking gratification altogether. But it is not impossible to put a limit on desires and learn to wait for the right time for gratification. When we act in the world by putting self-gratification first, we become selfish. We lose our judgment and develop sadness, depression, and pain. So along with limiting our desires, we have to limit the idea of gratification. In this way a harmony will be created between the inner and outer states, and the mind will be freed from discontentment, anger, fear, and pain.

35

---

*Happiness is a state of mind
where pleasure and pain
caused by attachment
do not exist.*

GENERALLY, THE MIND IS EITHER in pain or in pleasure. If we gain something we want, we get pleasure; and when that desire is obstructed, we get pain.
Sometimes, when the mind dwells between pleasure and pain, a state of happiness is experienced. As long as there is attachment, the mind will be pulled either way—to pleasure, or to pain. But when nonattachment develops, the mind achieves a satisfaction which is happiness. Mother Teresa in Calcutta is a good example. Her selfless work, with no attachment to her body, friends, or family, creates a state of happiness in her. She goes through many hardships of life and society, but the pain she endures strengthens her happiness.

36

*Life is like two big wheels
joined by a small wheel.
The past is a big
wheel, and so is the future.
The present is that moment
which joins
the past and the future.
If the present is made calm
and peaceful, it will
make the past and future
peaceful.*

PRESENT, PAST, AND FUTURE—These three together make a life cycle. In this lifetime the past is a big wheel that carries all the prints of past lives, and the future is also a vast, although unknown, wheel. The present is the smallest wheel—a moment that joins the past and the future. But our minds are trained to see a part of the past and a part of the future mixed with a moment of the present as one present. For example you say, "I am eating." Actually you have eaten some, which is the past, and you will eat some, which is the future, and only the moment when you are putting the food in your mouth is the present. That present, although but a moment, is continuously changing to the past. If that chain of moments passes in peace, then we are collecting a peaceful past. And that peaceful past is preparing a seed for the future to grow in the form of a tree of peace.

37

Limitation of desires is freedom of heart.

OUR DESIRES ARE THE CAUSE of attachment. We can't remove all desires so long as we are in the world. We live because there is a desire to live. We eat, sleep, and work to earn money for food because these things are necessary to keep the body alive. But our desires expand. We satisfy one desire and ten more come. Simultaneously the attachment, greed, anger, hate, and jealousy also increase. All these things put a veil over the heart, and the heart doesn't feel peace or happiness in the world. Life becomes a burden, and misery is seen everywhere. If desires are limited, the veils will start dropping away and the heart will be freed.

38

*Desire and imagination
are the cause of illusory reality,
the root of which penetrates
deeply into the memory.
The memory carries it
birth after birth.*

IN BOTH DESIRING AND IMAGINING, we create an illusory reality. That reality creates a deep print in the mind, which is called memory. That memory recreates desire, and the whole illusion starts over again with each birth.

If that memory is wiped out by some means, it will stop desire and imagination. Likewise, if the desire is removed, the memory gradually will get faint and disappear in course of time.

It is very hard to wipe out memory because it is very subtle; desire is its grosser form. It is less difficult to control desires; we have experienced them in the past and we continue to experience them all of the time. By watching the mind that is desiring, and by analyzing the desire and its effect, desires will get weaker. By developing awareness of the mind, one can practice reducing desires. This process is called *tapas,* or austerity.

39

*Giving up of desires
is austerity.*

ENJOYMENT OF DESIRES is a natural process in the evolution of the world. It's like a river that starts from the mountain, flows across the plains, and drops in the ocean. But when desires are stopped, it is like blocking the flow of water; the water hits the dam and breaks through. In the mind, when desires are restrained, the same thing happens: the desires get stronger and break through the idea of stopping them.

To strengthen the mind one observes mental and physical discipline: one eats in a particular way, sleeps for a particular length of time, dresses simply, and places limits on desires. This is called an austere life.

Austerity is nothing other than the giving up or limiting of our desires.

40

*The more you run after
the world, the more the world
will run away from you.
The more you run away from
the world, the more the world
will run after you.*

THE WORLD IS A CREATION of our desires.
There would be no world if desires ceased.
By fulfilling our desires, we increase the size of
our world. For example: one wants to get mar-
ried. Next one wants children; for them one needs a
house and a car. Still there will be discontentment. It
appears that no matter how many desires you run after
and are able to fulfill, you still remain discontented,
with the world still standing at arm's length.

On the other hand, if you remove all your desires,
your world will get smaller. But worldly pleasures, such
as name and fame, will start coming to you to allure
your mind. The more you try to remove your desires,
the more they present themselves.

In fulfilling desires there is discontentment, attachment, and greed, which lead to anger and fear of all
kinds. In removing desires there are tests. If you pass the
tests you attain peace.

41

*Peace of mind
is more important
than pleasure of the senses.*

THE SENSES ARE SERVANTS of the mind; they make a contact with the outer world for the mind. The mind gets addicted to the pleasures of the senses and forgets its real aim, which is peace. By getting involved in sensual pleasures, the mind gets angry, agitated, or depressed when those pleasures are obstructed or not obtained. If sensual pleasures are obtained, it develops greed, attachment, and possessiveness. In both cases peace of mind is disturbed and a person becomes a slave of his or her own senses.

Peace of mind can be obtained when the senses are under control, when the mind stops enjoying sensual pleasures, when the mind remains master of the senses.

42

*So long as we don't resist
unnecessary thoughts,
we will get caught more and
more in ignorance.*

IN THE MIND THERE ARE GOOD THOUGHTS, as well as bad thoughts. But because we are attached to this outer reality and our ego keeps a relationship with all of its objects—"It's mine. No, it's not mine. I need it. I don't like it"—the mind is always engaged in selfish thoughts. Where there is selfishness there is anger, fear, desire, jealousy, and so on—all of which strengthen selfishness. Even if the object is not there, its memory comes into the mind and at once the mind starts talking to itself—a process called day-dreaming.

If we don't stop all those unnecessary thoughts, there will be no time for good thoughts to come into the mind. The more unnecessary thoughts possess the mind, the more it gets confused and loses its power of discrimination. So, for a person who wants to attain peace and happiness in life, it is very important to stop unnecessary thoughts. At first one should develop awareness of those thoughts: how are they created, and how are they branching out? As soon as this awareness is developed, those unnecessary thoughts start falling away by themselves.

43

*If you want peace of mind,
renounce all those
thoughts of restlessness.*

THOUGHTS OF RESTLESSNESS are caused by desires and attachment, which in turn create anger, fear, hate, and jealousy. If we remove all those negative thoughts and cultivate positive thoughts in their places, then the mind will develop happiness, love, and peace.

THE UNSPOKEN LANGUAGE is trust, faith, devotion, and love. No spoken language is needed to express these qualities. When the mind is purified by silencing negative thought waves, positive qualities start developing.

The ears are the instrument for hearing a sound; where there is no sound, the ears have no function. But the heart is an instrument that feels the energy movement created by unspoken language.

A crow sits on a cow's back because there is a kind of trust; it never sits on a man's shoulder. In the case of the cow and the crow no language is needed because there is a mutual trust in their hearts.

A tribal archer named Eklabya had faith in a clay figure he made of his teacher. He learned the art of archery through that figure simply by faith. The clay figure had no way to use any language, but Eklabya could feel the energy of his teacher through it in his heart, and he attained the highest state of the art of archery.

The peace and love of sages who are completely devoted to God is felt by those who sit close to them. In the presence of Maharishi Ramana, people's questions were answered by his silence.

45

---

*Real human nature is
truth and love.
Mind and heart are the means
of its expression.*

NO MATTER HOW VIOLENT human beings
are, deep down there is a desire for peace.
If they are unhappy, angry, or afraid, they
know what caused it, and their real nature—
to seek for peace—will come up.

The faculty of thinking, reasoning, and understanding
is in the mind, and the faculty of expressing emotions is
in the heart, which is the seat of ego consciousness. So
when a person seeks for peace, it is expressed through
the mind by truthful thinking, truthful reasoning, and
truthful understanding. The search for peace is expressed
through the heart by removing selfishness, ego, and fear.

46

Motivation to bring peace to others is the cause of peace within.

EGO CONSCIOUSNESS is the cause of identification with the world. The first identification is "I am." The second identification is "I am this (or that"; "This is mine (or yours)." Everything is separated according to "mine" or "yours." By doing so, the mind develops attachment, greed, and violence. This creates pain in the person. It creates pain in one's family, friends, and in mankind in general.

This painful experience doesn't stop in one lifetime; it makes latent impressions in the mind and becomes first the cause of rebirth, and then guides all of life's actions by appearing as thoughts, desires, and tendencies. But if the nature of attachment, greed, and violence is changed by developing good qualities—love, compassion, nonviolence—the experience will act in the same way, but in a positive direction. It will create peace in the person; it will create peace for one's family, friends, and for mankind. The positive experience will also create a latent impression of peace, which will guide the next life in a positive direction. So any act that is giving peace to others is actually giving more peace to the doer.

Selfless service, like feeding the poor, taking care of the old, sick and homeless, being kind in action, speech, and thought, will bring peace to the human species.

Mother Teresa in India is a living proof of selfless service. She is giving peace to so many hearts, but her motivation to bring peace to others is the cause of her own peace. Anyone who meets her can feel that peace.

Chapter VI
SPIRITUAL MISCONCEPTIONS

47

One who waits for God to come remains waiting.

GOD IS NOT sitting somewhere in heaven. God is within us, within His creation. We don't see God because God has no form. If God were in a form, we could not say that God is infinite.

To attain God we must immediately start to purify ourselves. By purifying the mind, the veil of ignorance which hides that omnipresent, omnipotent, and omniscient energy is lifted.

A mountain climber will never reach the top if he or she sits at the base of the mountain and says, "Oh, I'll reach there if God wishes." God's wish, God's blessing, starts as soon as we start *purushartha* (effort to achieve God).

48

*One who depends on fate
or destiny and doesn't make
an effort remains sitting—
like one who sits
by the seashore waiting
for a pearl to wash up.*

KARMA IS ANY KIND OF ACTION—mental or physical—in which the ego is involved as a doer. That action makes a print in the mind which is called *samskara.* There are three kinds of *karma* or *samskara:* The first is called *samchit,* or collective *karma;* it is the unexhausted mass of *karmas* caused by constructive, destructive, and mixed actions of past births. They are carried in the memory and appear in the present birth in the form of desires. Secondly, there is *prarabdha,* the *karma* from the past which has ripened and bears fruit in the present life. *Prarabdha karma* determines one's natural tendencies and predispositions for action. It is familiarly referred to as fate. Thirdly, there is *agami,* the new *karma* which is continually being generated by present actions. These actions will bear fruit at some point in the future, sooner or later, depending upon the strength and nature of the deeds.

We know about our desires, both good and bad, and we can decide which desire should be fulfilled and which should not. We also know about the *karmas* happening in the present; but we don't know about those *karmas* which created fate. When something has already happened, only then can we say, "It was my fate," or "It was destined to happen."

If we depend on fate only and do not work to attain our goal, we cannot achieve anything. If one person should find a pearl at the seashore with no effort, it doesn't set the rule that others can also find one by doing nothing. If one sits by the seashore with the hope that some day fate will bring the pearl right in front of his or her feet, that person will remain sitting forever. On the other hand, one who depends on one's own efforts will practice diving deep into the sea and some day will develop the capability of bringing up pearls from the depths.

49

A picture of a fire looks like a fire, but it can't burn.

THEORY AND PRACTICE are two different things. Theoretical knowledge is like a picture of a fire that gives complete knowledge of the fire but doesn't give experience of its heat. For attaining experience, practice is the only way.

By seeing a map of London we can have understanding of roads, buildings, where factories are located, and the like, but we can't say, "I am in London." Being in London and knowing about London are two different things.

50

*Wondering about the source of
samskaras is a waste of time.
The important thing
is to pass every second of your
life in doing positive things.*

THE PRINTS OF GOOD AND BAD ACTIONS
in the mind, which we carry from one birth
to another, are called *samskaras*. *Samskaras* are
like seeds that germinate only when there is a
favorable soil but otherwise remain dormant. If one sees
one's pain and miseries and passes the time wondering
which *samskara* caused which pain, the pain won't be
cured; only time will be wasted in fantasizing about the
matter. If one develops positive qualities in action and
thought, a soil will develop in which positive *samskaras*
will germinate and negative *samskaras* will remain dormant. In this way a person can attain peace by simply
developing good qualities.

"He who has known for certain that adversity and
prosperity come in their own time through the effects
of past actions is ever contented, has all his senses under
control, and neither desires nor grieves." —*Ashtavakra
Samhita 11:3.*

51

*Those who say,
"I have to listen to my heart,"
and stop their efforts,
are listening to their desires
and not the truth.*

THE HEART IS AN EMOTIONAL MIND, and emotions are triggered by desires. When we say, "I have to listen to my heart and do whatever the heart says," we can very easily misguide ourselves because the language of the heart we are listening to is polluted by desires. But if the mind is purified and devotion and dispassion are attained, then the heart tells the truth.

The mind doesn't want any discipline; it always makes excuses to avoid it. So most people say, "I have to listen to my heart," and they stop their efforts to purify their minds. In this way they trick themselves and can't progress in their spiritual life.

52

Without reducing negative qualities, progress in spiritual life is as impossible as carrying water in a sieve.

NGER, HATE, JEALOUSY, ATTACHMENT, unkindness, and greed pull the mind toward the world. The mind can't see anything beyond self-interest. Every activity of the mind becomes selfish. It loses its purity and cannot feel the Self within. It loses its power of retaining God-consciousness and totally merges in the transient reality of the world. As long as all these holes of negative qualities are not sealed, God-consciousness cannot be retained in the mind—just as water can't be carried in a sieve.

53

*If the mind is not filled
with divine light, bliss, and
peace, then all the efforts
of yoga are useless.*

YOGA MEANS "UNION WITH GOD." This
union takes place when all the impurities like
attachment, egoism, and passion are removed
from the mind. Just as water mixes with water
and oil mixes with oil, in the same way a pure mind
filled with divine light, bliss, and peace loses its separate
identity and mixes with God—cosmic consciousness,
cosmic existence, and cosmic bliss.

Just as water and oil don't mix, an impure mind always
separates from all godly qualities. So long as an aspirant
doesn't try to cultivate good qualities—compassion, love,
equality, and selfless service—all yogic exercises will be
useless efforts.

54

*Acting out desires is not a
method of eliminating desires.*

WE GET HUNGRY; WE EAT FOOD and
our hunger goes away. This is the body's
natural process. It can't be applied, however, to our desires for objects. Desire, when
acted out, makes a print in the mind *(samskara)* of that
desire; then, when a favorable situation occurs, that
samskara causes the same desire to awaken. For example,
a man gets the desire to gamble. In gambling he loses all
of his money and leaves. After a few years he meets his
gambling friends, and again that desire comes up. If that
desire is not stopped altogether, the man will act it out
again.

Suppose one feels anger inside. If one acts it out by
beating a wall, it is not a real cure. First, the mind knows
that it is putting on an act, that the wall is not the real
object of its anger. Second, the mind also pretends that
the anger is gone. Third, it makes a *samskara* of that false
game. So the same act repeats again and again.

Refusing to fulfill your desires is austerity. Some
desires are important for living in the world, and those
are positive desires, such as the desire for food and
sleep. Some desires are created by the ignorance of the
mind, and those are negative desires, which need to be
eliminated.

55

*An aspirant can be in the
world like a boat on the water.
But if the world
is in the aspirant and water is
in the boat, both will sink.*

A **BOAT FLOATS** on the water; it is not attached to it. If the boat fills with water, it will sink. An aspirant is in the world, but the world, or desires, need not be in the aspirant. If the world fills the mind of an aspirant, he will sink, just like a boat filled with water. An aspirant should float on the world without creating attachments.

56

*You have to be truthful
to yourself in your actions,
thoughts, and speech
before you set out in search of
Ultimate Reality, Truth,
or Love.*

WE DON'T KNOW what Ultimate Reality, Truth, or Love is. We hear the theories and ideas of others and we believe in them. We read books and think, "that probably is the answer." On the one hand, it appears to be a big job to find out about Ultimate Reality; on the other hand, it is so easy to depend on others and follow them, accepting anything they say. Although we truthfully want to know what is beyond this physical reality, the mind chooses the easier course.

By leaning on others, we give them the whole responsibility, whether they are teacher, priest, saint, or religion. We forget completely that it's our own responsibility to discover and experience the Ultimate Reality. So we start talking about someone's teachings, we start thinking in a limited way according to the teachings or readings, and we even start acting as others. Our thoughts, speech, and actions become someone else's thing. It's like wearing blinders and following a sound.

As long as we lean on others, we can't be true to ourselves and we can't experience the Ultimate Reality, Truth, or Love. We have to use our own mind to think, our own words to express our experiences, and our own way of acting in the world.

57

To be true to yourself is a reality; being true to others can be an act.

A KIND OF TRUTHFULNESS can be used as self-advertisement. A preacher, teacher, or a leader confesses to having been bad, to having committed evil deeds, because those confessions advertise the person's truthfulness. If one is true to oneself, does one need to confess to having been bad? One who is true to oneself understands the meaning of truth and doesn't need to tell or prove how truthful he or she is.

There is a story in the *Mahabharata:* Dronacharya, the teacher of all princes, taught a lesson on truthfulness to his students. The next day he asked the princes if they understood truthfulness. Each prince raised his hand but one. His name was Yudhishthira. Dronacharya yelled angrily, "Why didn't you understand the lesson I taught? All of your brothers learned it. Tomorrow if you haven't learned your lesson you will be punished!" The next day Dronacharya again asked Yudhishthira if he had learned his lesson. The prince politely replied, "No, sir." Dronacharya beat him with a cane. The next day again Yudhishthira was punished. He very peacefully said, "Sir, I want more time to learn my lesson." This went on for several days, but Yudhishthira remained calm and peaceful. One day, when Dronacharya again asked if he had learned his lesson, Yudhishthira said, "Yes, sir. I was watching to see whether or not I was true to myself. As long as I was not truthful to myself, I did not want to say I had learned my lesson. It would be a lie." Dronacharya said, "My son, you are the only one who learned the lesson; all the others are simply putting on an act."

58

---

*Searching for God outside
is like looking for
your son who is sitting
on your shoulders.*

GOD IS NOT A PERSON living in a particular place outside of the world. Our search for God outside is simply a method of finding God inside.

A man who was a farmer was working in his garden with his son sitting on his shoulders. He forgot about his son and, when his work was over, he began to look around to see if his son had gone somewhere. He ran back home and asked his wife if their son had come home. The wife laughed and reminded him that their son was sitting on his shoulders. Outside search should remind us that we are forgetting that God is within us.

59

*So long as the limits
of religion are not broken,
one can't dissolve into God.*

A RELIGION TEACHES US HOW TO LIVE, how to pray, and offers a definition of God. A religion, however, can't create a feeling of God. This is attained by working within, where no religion can reach.

The world is divided by religions. Although the purpose of all religions is to attain the one God, each religion has given a name and form to God and, in this way, has put limits on the limitless God. Thus several Gods are created and the follower of each God rejects the God of others.

Universality will occur when we accept that there is one God who is worshiped with different names and forms by different religions.

A religious person is one who sees the similarities in all religions. All enlightened beings have broken the limitations of religion and have established a universality in their actions and teachings.

60

*A chess player loses
consciousnesss of the external
while creating
an internal world.*

IN MEDITATION THE MIND LOSES EXTERNAL
awareness and continuously flows toward one object. This flow of the mind is like projecting a film
of one picture on a screen: the picture will be seen
on the screen as motionless.

In playing chess a player also loses external awareness
and his or her mind is focused completely on the game.
But in this case, the mind doesn't retain one object; it
thinks of different possibilities and visualizes different
moves. Because the mind jumps to different objects, absorption in a game is not the same as meditation.

Chapter VII
SADHANA
SPIRITUAL ATTITUDES
and PRACTICES

61

If you work on Yoga, Yoga will work on you.

YOGA MEANS UNION—union of the individual soul with God. Here the word "Yoga" is used for methods through which the individual soul unites with God. "Working on Yoga" means practicing meditation and other methods which develop meditation, like *asana, pranayama, yama* and *niyama.* This practice should be done with faith, devotion, and continuous effort. One who practices in this manner attains *samadhi,* and the result of *samadhi* is attainment of truth, peace, higher knowledge, God. When this stage is attained, Yoga (union) will free one from the cycle of birth and death.

62

*Everyone's way of finding
God is a religion.
So there are as many religions
as there are individuals.*

RELIGION MEANS BELIEF in a divine power
that creates and rules the universe. This divine
power has no name or form. It has no limits—
no beginning and no end. It is beyond mental
conception, but a human mind tries to understand this
divine power by giving it a name, form, and attributes.

By saying "sky," the form of a concave blue dome
appears in the mind, but it is not real. In the same way,
when we say "divine power" or "God" different kinds
of figures or forms appear in the minds of individuals
according to their beliefs. No one sees exactly the same
form as others see. So the form of God in all minds is
different, even though the same methods, rules, and
form of God are accepted.

For some, selfless service is the way to find God; for
others love and compassion is the way. Some need to
renounce the world and meditate. Still others want to
surrender to that divine power and feel that everything
is taken care of by that power.

Each person has different thoughts, ideas, and imagination of God; so the way of finding God in the heart
is different for each. For example, a group of people is
worshiping God in a church, temple, or mosque; they
are chanting the same prayer, but their feelings toward
God are not the same. Each one's inner feeling for that
divine power is the religion for that individual. In this
way there are as many religions as there are individuals.

63

Truth and nonviolence are the two wings of an aspirant who takes off in search of liberation.

TO UNDERSTAND THE REAL NATURE of an object is truth. When the real nature of the body is realized, that is the truth of the body. When the real nature of thought is realized, that is the truth of the mind.

A mind affected with lust, fear, anger, greed, and attachment causes pain to others through thoughts or words, or by actual violence. Without truthfulness one can't observe nonviolence; and without nonviolence one can't observe truthfulness. They are separate, but always connected, like the two wings of a bird.

The mind is always affected by lust, desire, and anger. It always creates illusion and delusion. The confusion that results leads to violence and more untruthfulness. In this way, a being is trapped in the world. If, somehow, the mind is purified and one understands the truthfulness of life, then the mind will stop all kinds of violent acts. The aspirant will be released from the trap of the world and will take off to merge into the Supreme Self.

A hunter asks a sage sitting in his hut in the woods if he has seen a deer. The deer is hiding inside. If the sage says, "I did not see it," it's a lie. But if he says, "Yes, the deer is in the hut," the hunter will kill it. Here the truth of words is not seen; a universal truth is seen. The deer has the right to live, and the hunter has no right to take its life. The sage still remains truthful by saying, "I did not see the deer," because he saves himself from complicity in violence, which, in reality, is nontruth.

64

*The body is a vehicle
of the mind; and the mind
should take good care
of its vehicle.*

THE BODY CARRIES THE MIND WITHIN the brain mechanism. If the body dies, the brain mechanism also dies and the four faculties of the mind stop. The mind works through the senses and their instruments: ears, eyes, nose, etc. The mind is the charioteer of a chariot (body) with ten horses (senses). If this chariot and these horses are not taken care of properly, it can't run smoothly and won't last long. So the mind, which needs this chariot throughout its journey, should take good care of it by giving it pure food, enough exercise, inner and outer cleanliness, and by developing purity in action, thoughts, and speech.

65

The mind is like a child who, forbidden to do one thing, starts doing another.

ACTIVITY IS THE NATURE OF THE MIND; it can't remain idle. Thinking, desiring, feeling, working through the senses are its functions. If the mind is restrained from doing one thing, it never becomes inactive—it starts doing something else immediately. It is just like a child who crawls around grabbing things, throwing them, tearing them apart; if stopped, the child will crawl in another direction and start doing something else.

For a spiritual person it is important to control the mind. If its negative activities are gradually controlled, then it will automatically engage in positive activities. In this way the mind is withdrawn from worldly objects and is channeled toward God.

66

Silencing the mind is meditation.

THE MIND talks—it talks all the time, whether there is a listener or not. With people, it talks to them. In seclusion, it talks to itself. In sleep, it talks with dreams. All confusions in the mind arise only because the mind talks and never listens.

In meditation we first withdraw the mind from its attraction to different objects. Then we try to retain one object in the mind, which is God. Next we channel the mind toward that object. When the mind is absorbed in the object of meditation, its flow stops and the mind is completely silenced. That is a meditative state called *samadhi*.

Hitting the head with a hammer, or taking a strong drug, can also stop the mind, but it is not the same as silencing the mind. Crude methods may stop the mind from functioning normally through the senses (hearing, feeling, tasting, talking, smelling), but in the subconscious mind activity will continue. It is simply a state of unconsciousness and not a state of silence.

Genuine silence brings feelings of bliss, peace, and higher awareness; unconsciousness results in drowsiness, sadness, and unawareness.

67

Seeing the real
as separate from the unreal
is meditation.

ILLUSORY REALITY starts from our selfish desires—
we see things as real, just as in a dream everything
feels real. If we cultivate the habit of seeing things
without selfish desires, then things will appear as
they really are. The mind will gather the correct knowledge of things around us. In meditation, when the mind
is channeled to one object, it loses its selfish desire and
the object of meditation starts appearing in its real state.
Then true knowledge of the object is gathered.

68

*The chitta,
like fire without fuel,
calms down
when objects disappear.*

THE SENSE FACULTIES ARE CAPABLE OF perceiving their respective objects only when the mind desires to perceive. The sense faculties of the mind are hearing, touch, sight, taste, and smell; their sense organs are respectively ears, skin, eyes, tongue, and nostrils. Likewise, the object of each sense is sound, touch, form, taste, and odor.

When an object appears, it excites the whole brain mechanism in the following way: first the object is identified by the senses; the senses give a message to the mind *(manas)*; then the mind gives a message to the intellect *(buddhi)* to discriminate and differentiate; and at the same time the ego *(ahamkara)* establishes a relationship with the object, such as, "I am seeing this object," or "I am eating this apple." Then the intellect and ego send the message to *chitta*, or the subconscious part of the mind, to store the information in the form of *samskara*.

In this way an object stays in the *chitta* in the form of *samskara* until it again appears in the form of desire, or thought, and is passed on to the intellect and ego for its fulfillment. The intellect passes the information to the mind *(manas)*, and *manas*, which controls the senses, activates the senses to find the object.

So the object, which activates the mind's energy, is like fuel for fire. If the objects of the senses are decreased, then gradually the *chitta* will calm down—like fire without fuel—because the process of formation of desires and thoughts will be weakened.

69

Our thoughts are like strings which are attached to all the objects of world. Once these strings are removed, then all objects will be scattered like the beads of a broken rosary.

MIND IS NOT SEPARATE from its thought process. We identify with objects through our thoughts. Our senses relate to an object and send a message to the mind. In this way the mind establishes relationships among objects. For example, a car, a house, and a wife are three different objects, but a man is able to maintain a relationship with all three objects: my wife will live in this house; we will drive together in this car, and so on. If this kind of thought process is stopped, there will be no links between objects of the world, and the mind will remain in peace.

All the beads of a rosary are kept together by the string. All the beads move when one bead is moved. If the string is taken away, the beads will fall apart. The objects in the world will also scatter as soon as the mind stops its identifying function.

70

*The hero is not the one
who wins battles outside,
but the one who
conquers the mind.*

THE MIND IS THE CAUSE of attachments, ego, illusion, delusion, anger, fear, pleasure, and pain. All together they create ignorance. The soul is trapped within this ignorance, while the mind stands guard and fights if any attempt is made to rescue it. Winning battles outside is within the power of the mind, which can make plans and prepare physically and mentally to win the battle. But when the mind itself is opposing the rescue of the soul, the hardest battle is yet to be won. Ego, desires, and the thought process strengthen the mind. Only persistent practice of Yoga, accompanied by faith and devotion, can weaken these distractions. Then the mind can be conquered.

There is no greater victory than the victory over the mind because it liberates the soul from the cycle of birth and death. To weaken the mind, which is ruling the kingdom of illusion, we have to weaken its generals first. They are ego, desires, and unwanted thoughts. Ego is weakened by surrendering to God; desires are weakened by developing dispassion; and thoughts are weakened by *pranayama, pratyahara, dharana, dhyana,* and *samadhi.*

71

*There is no time limit
for burning impurities of the
mind; straw is ignited
as soon as a magnifying glass
is fixed against the sun.*

IF A MAGNIFYING GLASS IS FIXED AGAINST the sun to collect its rays on one point, it creates heat; and if there is straw beneath it, it catches fire. To fix the magnifying glass takes time. It should be at a perfect angle and a perfect distance from the straw, otherwise it will not collect the sun's rays at one point. Also there are disturbances, such as the hand shaking, or clouds covering the sun. We can't put a time limit on how long it takes to fix the glass, but it doesn't take long to make fire once the glass is fixed.

Exactly the same thing happens in the mind. The thing that takes time is setting the mind in the right direction. Once it is fixed, not much time is required to eliminate the mind's impurities. These impurities are *samskaras* that appear in the form of desire, attachment, and thoughts. No time limit can be set for training the mind to concentrate: some can do it in a short time, and some take years. But once the mind is trained to concentrate, the process of burning impurities *(samskaras)* goes quickly.

72

Time moves slowly for those who wait and quickly for those who don't.

TIME IS A MEASUREMENT OF SPACE. Time itself has no reality, no existence; the earth and the moon are moving in relation to the sun, and from this we created the time on our clocks. Although clock time is a regular and consistent measurement, our perception of time changes according to our activities and expectations. For example: You are expecting your friend to come at 4:30, but he doesn't show up. Every minute you are waiting feels so long. When he comes you say, "Why did you take such a long time?", although he was only ten minutes late.

In spiritual life we are talking about the time it takes to get free from the ignorance which causes pain, unhappiness, and confusion in our lives. Time moves slowly for those who think that some day they will try to get out of the world. They are like a man who is digging a ditch and periodically stops digging; the time of completing the ditch will obviously be longer. But for one who is continuously working hard to remove ignorance, the time of achieving the goal will move quickly. In simple words, one who is working hard to attain peace will attain peace faster than those who are not working hard.

73

Sitting in silence will not go to waste; some day you will reap the harvest of peace.

SILENCE IS AN AUSTERITY OF SPEECH in the gross body. In the subtle body it is an austerity of the desire to speak. Silence is practiced for three purposes: for preservation of *prana,* or vital energy, for silencing the mind, or inner chatting, and for avoiding abusive language.

When we talk, we talk while exhaling; the more we talk, the more we have to exhale. The more we exhale, the more physical energy we lose. So the first effect of silence on the gross body is a reduction of the energy used and a subsequent increase in the span of life.

Our mind talks all of the time, whether there is someone else to converse with or not. When one is alone, the mind still creates some company in its imagination and starts a conversation. But if one wants to sit in silence, the mind's talking will not be welcome. At first the mind will put up a resistance because there is a desire to talk; but gradually the desire will decrease, the resistance will weaken, and inner talking will lessen. When all inner talking is stopped, the mind will dwell in peace.

*Effort is necessary
so long as the ego is alive.
If the ego is dead,
efforts cease to exist.*

EGO AND EFFORT ARE RELATED: "I am doing this" equals ego of individuality. Ego is life. In the world where we are born, we can't function without the ego of being. That ego is the root cause of effort. The ego wants to exist and for existence effort is necessary.

The ego, which is very important for our existence in the world, is also very important for pulling us out of the world. To get out of the world we need effort. Again we have to use the same "I" which wants to get out of the world. But that same ego becomes a hindrance when the mind is purified and the aspirant begins to see the path clearly. That path is steep and the aspirant starts sliding down it, but the ego gets afraid and tries to pull him back.

If the ego is somehow completely removed at that stage, then the sliding process, which is an effortless effort, will not stop. This sliding action is not an effort because there is no doer; although the action never stops, there is no one who claims that "I am doing it."

If the culprit is dead, who will get the sentence? When the ego is dead, neither the mind nor the individual self can be blamed for any kind of effort. The mind without the ego loses its power of identification with the world, and the individual self without the ego is the pure Self, simply "I."

75

*There is no failure
on the spiritual path because
the soul reincarnates
again and again
until liberation is attained.*

A SOUL TAKES BIRTH WITHIN A BODY TO experience enjoyment and pain, and to get liberation from those experiences—which themselves create latent impressions and are the cause of birth and rebirth.

In the ordinary course, the process of experience and liberation goes on in its natural way. The mind gets attached to objects; then it goes through different kinds of pain and tries to get out of that pain. It liberates itself from one object and gets attached to another. In this way enjoyments, pleasure, pain, and liberation repeat continuously and it is called life.

There is one larger cycle in which the object of attachment is not any outer object, but life itself. The mind is attached to the body and wants to live with that body forever. This causes pain, which is created by the ignorance of the mind. The soul is indirectly connected with this ignorance because the mind thinks it is the soul as well as the body.

As a spiritual aspirant, one tries to free oneself from attachment to outer objects. When one removes the attachment to an object, one feels success; but if one can't remove that attachment, one feels failure. Actually the question of failure doesn't arise because the mind is not losing its purpose of experience and liberation. It still goes on; but one does not get much closer to liberation because the mind keeps falling back to attachment.

Still, an unconscious effort goes on because the embodied soul's purpose is to experience and get liberation from those experiences. Again the aspirant will start to make a conscious effort. In this way conscious effort and unconscious effort go on until the soul is liberated from its purpose of experience of enjoyments.

Chapter VIII
LIBERATION
DISPASSION

76

Ignorance alone causes suffering; knowledge alone removes it.

THE CAUSE OF SUFFERING is ignorance, which takes the form of desire, fear, anger, attachment, or aversion. We see everything according to our desires, and we get attached to the idea that "it is mine," or "it is not yet mine." A fear of losing the object develops, and the mind uses anger as a defensive mechanism.

For us, every object or person is nothing more than our desires. These desires create a veil over our mind and block our vision from seeing the object or person in its natural way.

Knowledge arises when the mind develops awareness of its ignorance. The mind then sees how the desires, fear, and anger cause suffering, and it tries to remove the attachment. Gradually the mind develops dispassion, which ends all the suffering.

77

Experience is the best teacher; it shows the path for the future.

A BABY TAKES BIRTH AND GROWS. His ego-sense develops and he tries to experience his limits. He tests various objects and finds out how things are affecting him. His experiences in the world teach him the difference between good and bad, hot and cold, day and night, and so on.

When the child gets bigger he copies his parents. He listens to them and accepts what they say; but still his real learning comes from his own experience. That a candle flame burns can be accepted by a child from the words of his parents, but without experience there can't be real learning and complete acceptance. So the child tests and feels the heat, and his mind accepts that all burning flames are hot and can hurt him. He doesn't need to touch wood fire, gas heater, or oil lamp. One experience taught him a complete lesson.

In this way one experience covers a vast range of learning. There is a story about an *avadhuta* (wandering saint) who was questioned about how he got such vast knowledge. The *avadhuta* replied that he had twenty-four teachers. He said:

" (1) From earth I learned forebearance. (2) From air I learned nonattachment: the air carries good and bad odors but remains unaffected. (3) From the all-pervading ether I learned the omnipresence of *Atman* (soul) in the animate and in the inanimate. (4) From water I learned the purifying effect of a sage: a sage purifies anyone who reveres him, like water that purifies and soothes. (5) From fire I learned how to burn the evils of others: a fire consumes anything you throw in it, while remaining unaffected. (6) From the moon I learned the revolving of time: although the moon looks big at times and small at other times, it really never changes. In the same way, time, which causes birth and death, doesn't affect the *Atman*. (7) From the sun I learned the omnipresence of *Atman*: as the sun reflects in many water pots, so the *Atman* reflects in each and every individual. (8) From a family of pigeons I learned about attachment: when the baby pigeons were trapped, the mother pigeon also jumped into the trap, and then the father pigeon too. In this way, the whole family was killed due to their attachment to each other. One who is attached to the world remains trapped in the cycle of birth and death. (9) From a python I learned to remain satisfied: a python eats whatever comes to him; he remains satisfied and doesn't struggle for more food. (10) From the ocean I learned to remain unchanged: it is calm and placid, whether rivers are flooded or dried up. Similarly, the wise man remains calm and unchanged amidst the opposites of life. (11) From the moth I learned the deadliness of attraction: her attraction to the flame of a lamp is uncontrollable and she kills herself. Similarly, a fool is destroyed by attraction to lust and gold. (12) From an elephant I learned not to look with lustful eyes upon anyone: an elephant gets trapped by his lustful desire when he sees a female elephant in a pit. (13) From a bee I learned not to hoard: a bee hoards honey and one day it gets destroyed by the honey collectors. In the same way, one who hoards wealth will be destroyed. From honey gatherers I learned not to profit from another's hoarded wealth: they steal honey from the bee hives and make a business out of it. Neither do they enjoy the honey themselves, nor do they let the bees enjoy it. (14) From a deer I learned not to get trapped by listening to sensual music: a deer, being enamored of sweet sounds, falls into the snare. (15) From a fish I learned not to get destroyed by taste: a fish is hooked because of the taste of a worm. (16) From Pingala, a prostitute, I learned to find happiness within myself. Pingala waited for a rich lover to come to her; when midnight passed she got tired and impatient. She felt disgust within herself, and she realized her folly, her lack of self-control, her greed for money, and her expectation of finding happiness from a man. She realized that God is the true lover and that He is eternal and always near one. (17) From an osprey I learned about attachment which leads to miseries. When an osprey carries a piece of flesh in his mouth, stronger birds attack him. As long as the flesh is in his mouth he is attacked; as soon as he gives up the piece of flesh he becomes free and happy. (18) Like a child, I learned to be happy and carefree. Having no attachment to family and possessions, I take delight in the contemplation of the Self and wander about freely. (19) I learned from a maiden that only by being solitary can one be saved from quarrels and gossip. A young man wanted to marry a maiden and went to see her. She was husking paddy and her conch bracelets were making sounds while she was husking. She did not want

the man to know that she was engaged in such a menial task, so she took off the bracelets one by one until two remained on each wrist. They, too, made a sound, so she took one off from each hand. From single bracelets there was no sound. Where many dwell in one place, there is noise and quarreling. Even with two people there may be harmful gossip. Therefore it is better for one to be solitary, like a single bracelet on either arm of the maiden.

(20) From an arrowmaker I learned to concentrate on my task: the arrowmaker is so concentrated while making arrows that he loses outside awareness and rises above the tumult of the subjective and objective worlds. (21) From a snake I learned not to bind myself with a home: a snake occupies holes made by others and lives happily. (22) From a spider I learned that the eternal, unchangeable Lord, who has no form or attributes, who is absolute knowledge and absolute bliss, evolves the whole universe out of Himself, plays with it, and again withdraws it into Himself, as a spider weaves its thread out of its own mouth, plays with it, and then again withdraws it into itself. (23) From vramarkita (an insect) I learned that a man becomes what he dwells on, whether it be love, or hate, or fear. It is like a cockroach who develops fear when attacked by a vramarkita; he thinks about the vramarkita and becomes one with it. (24) From my own body, which is subject to birth and death and is the cause of suffering and misery, I have awakened within myself dispassion and discrimination. Knowing myself separate from the body, I have learned to meditate on the eternal Truth."

78

What's the purpose of the mind?

THE MIND HAS A PURPOSE: to free itself from its own creation, which is nothing but *maya,* or illusion.

When this illusion gets known for what it is, the mind then develops dispassion toward its own creation. That dispassion eliminates the illusion and, finally, itself. The process is like that of purifying molten bronze: charcoal powder is thrown into the liquid bronze; it purifies the bronze and then burns itself up. There remains only pure bronze.

Dispassion is that charcoal powder which purifies the mind. When the mind is completely purified, it becomes pure consciousness. In that state no dispassion is needed, so it eliminates itself also.

79

One becomes fit for liberation only when extreme desire for liberation is attained.

EXTREME DESIRE FOR LIBERATION is the cause of creating dispassion for the world. The mind develops distaste for worldly enjoyments. Worldly objects lose their apparent reality and the mind reverses its outward flow, turning toward its origin, which is God.

In fact, extreme desire for liberation is no different than extreme dispassion. In the state of extreme dispassion the mind rejects everything. All desires, thoughts, and activities are rejected, and the mind dissolves into nothingness. Then a state of *Nirbija Samadhi** is gained, which establishes non-duality, and the aspirant attains complete liberation.

---

* *Samadhi* without seed, or object.

80

*Dispassion comes
when the mind develops
nonattachment to objects
of the senses.*

OUR MIND DEVELOPS attachment through the senses. The mind alone can't enjoy anything; for enjoyment it needs instruments of enjoyment, which are the senses. When an object is enjoyed by the mind, attachment and possessiveness, or repulsion and hate, are created. In both cases the mind relates to an object. If the mind stops enjoying objects through the senses—for example, one eats to live and not to enjoy the food—it develops dispassion for objects.

The body is the main object with which the senses identify. When this body consciousness is stopped, the mind dwells in extreme dispassion.

81

*Reach out to serve others,
but watch out
for your self-interest.*

ERVING OTHERS WITHOUT SELF-INTEREST is a way of purifying the mind. If we expect others to come and seek our help, then it's our ego. We have to eliminate that ego by reaching out to those who are sick, or poor, or in pain. We have to listen to their stories and try our best to help them.

In selfless service we start with a good intention, but we have our own desires, needs, and expectations. Always the mind falls back and questions, "What am I getting by serving others—name, fame, power?" If the mind is aware of those very subtle desires and tries to remove them whenever they appear, then the mind attains a state of satisfaction, contentment, and peace. It eliminates the ego of being a doer, and the mind becomes very pure and dispassionate toward the world. It's a state of complete surrender to God.

Chapter IX
LIBERATION
AWAKENING *and* RELEASE

82

Ignorance exists as long as the illusion of the world is not completely forgotten.

OUR DESIRES CREATE an illusory form in the world. Based on desire we see a form, feel it, enjoy it, or hate it. Just as the sky is seen as blue and concave, although that is not the real form of the sky, in the same way the ignorant mind sees all forms. They are, however, merely illusions created by the desires. As long as the world is seen in its illusory form, ignorance exists in the mind. When wisdom dawns, this ignorance disappears, just as darkness disappears when the sun comes up.

83

*Guru is one
who is not in bondage;
disciple is one
who is in ignorance.*

IT IS OUR MIND THAT CREATES CONFUSION and entraps itself by its own created web, so we can say that the mind is the disciple. The Self is not in bondage; it is ever free and omnipresent, omnipotent, and omniscient, so we can call the Self the guru. The disciple wants to be released from the pain and suffering created by ignorance, but when the mind is not capable of receiving the Truth, the guru can't resort to force.

The mind, however, can develop the capability of receiving the Truth by cultivating good qualities and single-mindedness in actions and thoughts. As long as the mind is disturbed by desire, fear, pleasure, and pain, it sees nothing but itself in everything. In other words, everything outside is our mind in a disturbed state. When it is not disturbed, there is perfect peace and the disciple (mind) is liberated from its web of ignorance.

84

We act in the world
by self-programming and
we can get out of the world
by self-programming.

IN ALL OUR ACTIONS, thoughts, and words, ego sense is involved. The mind is so quick to make a complete program whenever we have to do something. It orders the senses, it gets information through the senses, it finds out how some of our acts relate to the ego sense. Our desires, thoughts, needs, attachment, pleasure, pain are all self-programmed. The mind creates all those things and acts out that program. In the same way, the mind can develop non-attachment, dispassion, and egolessness by self-programming. The mind says there is no reality in the world, and then the mind starts seeing and feeling it through the senses. The ego sense starts separating from external objects. In this way, when the ego sense completely separates from objects, the world disappears from the mind and one releases oneself from the cycle of birth and death.

85

Understand bondage in life
before seeking liberation.

THE BODY IS BONDAGE because it is subject
to conditions of space, time, and causation.
Birth and rebirth are caused by the result of
deeds in previous lives. In this way deeds and
their result make a chain of *karma* (action) and *samskara*
(prints of actions in the mind) which imprisons the soul
in a cycle of birth and death.

In a prison all are prisoners, but some are allowed to
go out and work and some have to stay behind bars. A
body is like that prison. But in a human body the pris-
oner has some freedom. That freedom is due to the superior mind a human being possesses. In other bodies—
animals, birds, insects—the soul is imprisoned in the same
way, but there is no freedom; the creatures live and die
just as they are supposed to live and die.

What makes this prison? Our attachment to the body,
desire for enjoyment, and wrong identification with the
body are the cause of the body becoming the soul's
prison.

The body is constituted of five elements—earth, water,
fire, air, and ether—and it is ruled by the spirit. There is
a bridge between matter, or gross body, and the spirit.
That bridge is the energy body (the subtle body). The
subtle body uses the gross body as an instrument in all
actions, such as smelling, tasting, seeing, touching, hearing. Although the spirit is behind all these actions, the
wrong identification starts here, where the gross body
and the subtle body together become real and the spirit
is completely forgotten. It is a limited reality, however,
limited in its thinking and acting.

One who starts seeing this limitation of the body seeks for liberation. Liberation is simply right identification with the Self. Knowledge of the Self is the direct cause of liberation.

The Self, which is real existence in a human being, is omnipresent, omniscient, and omnipotent. It reveals itself as soon as it is identified as the Self. If a man finds a coin on the street and thinks it is a brass coin, in his

mind there is not much value in it; but when someone tells him it is a gold coin, its value is revealed by itself. The coin was always a gold coin, but by wrong identification it had no value. By right identification that ignorance is wiped out and real value is revealed.

So we are always liberated if we only know what bondage is.

86

*Before attaining liberation,
you have to forget
all you have learned.
Liberation
is beyond learning.*

ALL THAT WE LEARN IS ABOUT THE WORLD and for the world. On the one hand, without learning about the world we can't function in it; but on the other hand, the knowledge of the world creates attachment to it. We don't want to lose our world, so we become afraid. That fear of losing the world gives rise to anger. We are always prepared to defend our "rights" if someone, knowingly or unknowingly, comes to take away our world. In this way, the mind is always engaged in the fear of losing and in the anger of defending. We have no time to see what is beyond our fear and anger.

To attain liberation, we have to remove all the elements which are tying us down: the worldly knowledge that creates attachment, the attachment that creates fear, the fear that gives rise to anger—the anger that takes various forms, like hate, jealousy, cruelty—and on and on.

87

---

*Life is for learning
and the world is our school.
Doing your homework
every day
brings liberation.*

THE PURPOSE OF LIFE is twofold: *bhoga,* or experience, and *apavarga,* or liberation. In order to renounce something, you have to have it first. In the same way, in order to achieve liberation you have to have experience from which you must get liberated.

Your life span is from the birth of your soul to its liberation. The world is like a school and in the course of your life span you are experiencing or learning something every second. Your experience of bad things warns you against repeating them. And if you remember all the good things you experience in your day-to-day life—which is like homework—then your mind will be purified and your attachment to the world will be reduced.

When the mind is totally non-attached to all experiences, their memories, and their results—which is liberation itself—then liberation of the soul is attained.

88

*Pleasure, pain, love, hate,
anger, fear are born with the
mind and are fed by the mind.
They exist as long as
the mind exists.
When pure consciousness
dawns, the mind
with its products disappears.*

THE MIND IS THE MASTER OF THE BODY.
Through the body the mind expresses all
emotions, feelings, and desires. Pleasure, pain,
love, hate are caused by the mind and identified by the mind. When the mind is in deep sleep or a
faint, those things are not identified. If those qualifica-
tions were in the Self, they would be omnipresent, just
like the Self which continues to exist in deep sleep or
faint.

When the mind is purified by the practice of *samadhi*,
it transforms into higher consciousness. In that pure
state of consciousness, all the productions of the mind
cease to manifest.

89

*A dream and the world
are both real
until one wakes up.*

A DREAM IS MANIFESTED BY desire, imagination, and memory. Desire has to do with the present, imagination is a process of the future, and memory comes from the past. In this way all three—present, past, and future—are in a dream.

The world is also created in the same way. There is one physical object, but that object is seen according to our desires, we imagine how it relates to us, and we keep its memory. The physical object is a reality, but the way the mind has given it a particular shape according to our desires, the way the mind has established a relationship with the object and created attachment to it, and the way the mind keeps its memory are all unreal and simply created in the mind.

Dream reality remains while one is asleep; as soon as one wakes up the dream reality vanishes. In the same way, as long as the mind is projecting its desires and attachment onto objects, we are dreaming the world as if real. As soon as the mind stops this projection we wake up in the world and we see the reality.

90

---

*The mind flies like a bird
in the sky of desires
until it comes under the attack
of a hawk, or jnana.*

THE SKY IS *AJNANA* or ignorance. In this ignorance the mind flies like a bird from one
desire to another. It hovers high up in the sky,
looking for new desires, and sometimes dives
for a particular desire without seeing the consequences.

Jnana, or knowledge of the truth, is like a hawk. As
soon as this hawk starts hovering, the bird (mind) stops
its flight (becomes motionless), or gets attacked. In both
cases the mind loses its independence and disappears.

91

*A silkworm makes a net of silk
and traps herself.
Similarly, an individual soul
makes a net of plans
and desires in the form
of the world and unwittingly
imprisons herself.
When the traps are broken,
both fly away.*

THE SOUL IS LIMITLESS existence, consciousness, and bliss. Due to the ego sense, which is a bridge between the soul and the world, all of our *samskaras* envelop the soul and hide its real nature. Then the soul appears as if it is acting, feeling pain and pleasure, and so on. This is a net of attachment around the soul. The soul is seen in the state of *bhoga*, or worldly enjoyment. It makes its own trap, like the silkworm, which weaves a trap of its own saliva and imprisons itself. When the net of attachment is broken, the ego sense dissolves into the soul. Then the soul realizes its own nature—existence, consciousness, and bliss. All limitations are broken and, like a butterfly, the soul flies to her abode, which is God.

Chapter X
LIBERATION
BEYOND DEATH

92

Death is a reality which can't be avoided, halted, or altered.

THE WORD "DEATH" IS A SYMBOL of fear. It gives us the idea that we will lose this reality, we will cease to exist. No longer a being, we will be unable to think or enjoy the senses and the miracles of this world. We have a deep fear of permanent, dreamless, consciousless sleep, of all of "this" ending.

What is death? Complete forgetfulness of past identities is death—when you are no longer that person in that body. In the state of *Asamprajnata Samadhi*, there is also death of the former person, because the former person ceases to exist in that body. But for witnesses of that *samadhi*, it is not death because they only identify the person with that body.

Death is a reality. For that reason, in Hinduism the god of death is named Dharma Raj, lord of *dharma*, or the law of life.

We all know that one who takes birth will surely die, but we don't want to see it, hear about it, or feel it. That is only because our mind dwells in the ignorance of "I am this body." We want to live eternally, no matter how much pain and misery is incurred in life.

The fear of death pervades all three periods of time: present, past, and future. In the present it manifests as fear of losing this reality; in the past there are memories of previous deaths; and in the future there is fear of the unknown.

93

Anger and fear are two sides of the same coin.

ANGER IS A MEANS OF SELF-DEFENSE against fear. Fear is the cause of anger, and fear of death is the root cause of all fears. So long as a person is afraid of death, all other fears will be present. Whenever threatened by anything, one will express anger as a self-defense against fear.

A snake will not attack as long as its life is not threatened. A crow sits on the back of a cow and not on a man. A saint who has accepted death as a part of life shows no anger in words, thought, or actions; all creatures of the jungle sit around the saint without fear.

94

Fear of death is the root of all fears. One who has removed that fear is liberated.

FEAR IS INHERITED FROM THE DAY LIFE energy takes an individual form. As soon as a body is formed, a natural desire to live is also formed. But no one can live forever because immortality is against the law of nature. So the fear of death arises. As the living form evolves, ego consciousness becomes stronger and the fear of death increases. This is a fear of the unknown; we don't know what is going to happen and so we are always afraid. We are afraid of losing what we have and we are afraid of things that do not support our individuality.

On the one hand, fear is a big block to finding peace, love, and liberation; on the other hand, it is a cause of motivating a person to seek liberation. When we know that we are not immortal we feel limited, helpless, and afraid. We seek a refuge where fear will not haunt us. We seek a support, so we create a form of God in our mind and surrender to that God.

Although that God is simply a mental creation, it is helping us in various ways. First, the mind that carries the memory of fear of the unknown is weakened by our faith in God. Second, we feel supported by God, and our fear, which sits like a mountain on our path, gets smaller. Third, it develops faith and devotion and increases the desire to get liberation. Fourth, the mind starts seeing the world as unreal—simply created as real in our mind by our desires, fears, ego, and attachment. This state of dispassionate mind becomes fit for liberation.

95

When the soul
leaves the physical body,
it is called death;
when the soul leaves the
subtle body,
it is called liberation.

A BEING LIVES IN THREE BODIES. These three bodies are like sheaths, one inside the other. The first body is called the gross body. We can see this body, touch it, and give it a name; and we say, "It is my body," or "It is me." Inside that gross body there is another body called the subtle body. It is an energy body that can't be seen by the eyes or felt by the hands. All of the activities of the gross body—hearing, seeing, touching, feeling, thinking, desiring, as well as the attachments and aversions it forms—are, in fact, due to the energies of the subtle body; the gross body is simply its instrument. The third body is the causal body. It is located within the subtle body, is even more intangible, and is the cause of both the subtle and the gross bodies.

The soul, self, or spirit resides in all three bodies and witnesses all of their activities. When the soul leaves the gross body, it doesn't leave alone; the causal and subtle bodies in seed form go with the soul. It means that all potential energies become dormant. At this stage we say the person is dead. Yes, the gross body is dead, but still the two other bodies are with the soul. Buried in their seed form is the desire to enjoy the objects of the senses. For this a physical body is needed, so the soul is again pulled back to a new physical form.

If somehow the mind is stopped from desiring sense objects—even the desire to live—the mind develops supreme dispassion. It stops all of its functions, such as thinking, desiring, feeling "I am this (or that)." It develops a high stage of *samadhi*. In that stage the soul leaves the subtle body.

Throughout life the soul is bound to the subtle body by the chains of desires, egoism, and attachment to life itself. When these chains are broken, the subtle body dies, and the causal body merges into *prakriti*, original nature. It is called liberation.

96

*By simply eliminating desires
the illusion of the world
is eliminated, and one is freed
from the cycle
of birth and death.*

OUR DESIRES ARE THE CAUSE OF GIVING a particular form to an object and creating a relationship with it. When our desires change, the form of an object changes accordingly, as well as our relationship to the object. For example, a man has a house. If anything is broken, he repairs it. He decorates the house and enjoys its beauty. One day he sells the house. Now his desire and attachment to the house are changed: he will not enjoy it, even if the new owner has decorated it more beautifully; he will not worry if the house falls down. So what we see in an object is not a reality but an illusion projected by our desires. This illusion creates ignorance, pain, and attachment. If desires are eliminated, then one can identify with the world in its real form.

Birth and death are also an illusion. We identify ourselves with the body and when a body dies, we think that the real person in that body has also died. Actually, the soul never dies and never reincarnates—only its vehicle, a physical form, dies and takes birth again. This truth is revealed when the mind is freed from desires and one attains real knowledge—identification with the Self where there is no birth or death.

97

*Purified mind is the healer
of the body,
of birth, and of death.*

THE MIND AND THE BODY are very closely related. In the body each cell keeps the consciousness of the mind as its own. Just as one God shines in the form of countless individual souls, one mind shines in each cell of the body.

Sickness of the body causes fear in the mind. That fear originates from the experience of death in past lives.

Birth is caused by the mind's attachment. We are attached to the body and want to remain in that body forever.

Death is nothing but the mind's ignorance. The body becomes so real to us that we identify only with that body and completely forget past identities. When the mind is purified, ignorance, desire, and fear of death are eliminated, and a person is freed from sickness, birth, and death.

98

---

*Truth is revealed
when the Self becomes one
with God.*

IGNORANCE STARTS WHEN THE SELF starts forgetting its source (God). This is the only ignorance that exists. All other forms of ignorance are based on this.

The first step of illusion is egoism: "I am this," "I am that." The Self starts identifying with a form; then the form is identified with a name, shape, and size in space and time. When this form acts, it makes *samskaras*. Those *samskaras* cover the Self, layer after layer, and close off the vision of the Self completely.

When the layers of *samskaras* are removed—like layers of an onion—there remains only one thing and that is God. When the Self realizes, "I am no other than God," that is the Truth.

Chapter XI
LIBERATION
SELF-REALIZATION

99

*A person knows who he is,
who he was, and who he will be
only when the mind
becomes pure and calm.*

THOUGHTS IN THE MIND ARE BASED ON
desires. Desire is the cause of attachment,
and attachment is the cause of all pain.

The joy or sorrow attained by attraction of the
senses to an object is called attachment. Attachment
destroys the discriminative power of the mind, and the
result is ignorance. Ignorance creates delusion, which
covers the knowledge of the Self. This condition is like
stirring water in a pond, making it so muddy that one
can't see the bottom.

The Self has all knowledge: the past, present, and future are one in the Self. When the mind is purified, all
mental modifications are stopped and one becomes
perfectly tranquil, free from desires and aversions, and
identification with the Self is established. That is liberation where past, present, and future become one.

In Yoga Sutra 2:39 Patanjali says: "Being confirmed
in non-possessiveness, the knowledge of how and from
where birth comes arises." Possessiveness is the sense of
"my and mine." This is the greatest impurity of the
mind and it leads to ignorance. When this impurity of
possessiveness is wiped out, then all of time begins to
shine by itself, and a yogi clearly sees his or her past,
present, and future lives.

100

*Remove all the selves we create
and what remains
will be identified as real Self.*

THE WORD "I" IS AN INDICATOR OF SELF. "I am happy"—this is a self who is happy. "I am sad"—another self who is sad. "I am hungry, I am attached, I need money, I am hurt"— all these different selves are appearing in the mind, and all are simply mind-body experiences which are identified as "I." If we remove all these concepts of "I" which come into the mind in different ways, then what will remain? Something beyond the mind, beyond the sense of individuality, which is the real Self.

101

Learned is one who can distinguish between the Self and the mind. Ignorant is one who identifies with the body.

THE SELF IS TRUTH, unchangeable and eternally free, but it appears to be bound in grief and delusion, happiness and misery, birth and death.

The mind is the instrumental factor in covering the Self with its own illusion. It gives objects false shapes, forms, or identities according to desires and projections, and it appears as a Self-in-itself.

When one has limited oneself to the body-mind complex and thinks that when the body sleeps the Self is asleep, that when the body dies the Self dies, one is identifying with nothing but a body of ignorance.

When the mind is purified and not disturbed or confused by its own thought waves, then only can an aspirant recognize the Self as separate from the mind. That is called attainment of *viveka khyati,* or discriminative knowledge of Self and non-Self.

102

*Reflection of the Self
on chitta is consciousness,
and the Self is realized by
its own reflection.*

THE SELF IS NOT CHITTA, but the activities in *chitta* are created by the presence of the Self. When a mirror is turned to the sun, it creates heat. It is the sun that creates heat—the mirror has no energy of its own. Only when the sun's reflection falls on the mirror and that reflection focuses on objects is heat felt. In the same way, the Self is a sun and the *chitta* is a mirror.

The Self can't be identified as long as the *chitta* is not pure. An impure *chitta* creates the ignorance that the *chitta* itself is the Self; we cannot think of anything beyond the *chitta*. When the *chitta* is purified, however, the reflection of the Self on the *chitta* starts getting clear. That clarity of reflection of the Self on *chitta* is called higher consciousness. Only through that consciousness is the Self realized.

103

The Self is known by its own light, as the sun is seen by its own light.

WHEN THERE IS NO SUN, IT IS DARK, and in that darkness nothing is seen. When the sun comes up, its light spreads all around and everything is seen, including the disk of the sun and its rays. In the same way, when the Self is not known there is ignorance. In that ignorance we don't see anything as it is. But when the Self is identified as separate from the body, then everything is seen as it is, including the Self.

Chapter XII
LIBERATION
UNION with GOD

104

Duality exists as long as God is not identified within.

A PITCHER HOLDING WATER FLOATS in the ocean and keeps its separate identity. Likewise, a being exists in duality as long as there is the ego of separateness: "I am this body, with this name, and this religion."

When the pitcher is broken, the water inside it disappears into the water of the ocean. There is no existence of the pitcher and no separation of water—there remains only ocean. In the same way, when the ego that identifies with the body and makes a separateness is broken, the ego *(ahamkara)* dissolves into the Self *(asmita,* or beingness). Actually, the ego comes from the same source as the Self. The Self in the body is the existence of God within. As long as God is not identified within, we (the ego-self) will remain separate from the true Self (God).

105

As soon as one knows one's Self, God will be known.

OUR MIND IS COVERED BY THE WRONG knowledge, "I am this body-mind complex," "I am this personality." We never feel that the "I" in this body is separate from the body. What is that "I"? Is it a part of the mind? Is it an ego? Or is it something else? When this question is solved, then one can identify with the Self.

The Self, which takes the body as an abode, is changeless, immortal, beyond time and space, and a witness. It is embodied only so long as it is not identified as separate from the body. As soon as it is identified as separate, it is also identified as omnipresent, omnipotent, and omniscient, which are the qualities of God.

106

Complete absorption in God comes when manas, buddhi, ahamkara, and chitta are separated from the Self. That state is called kaivalya (perfect isolation).

MANAS, BUDDHI, AHAMKARA, CHITTA are four parts of the whole mind. *Manas* is the recording faculty, which receives and transmits information through the senses. *Buddhi* is the discriminative faculty, which separates all information. *Ahamkara* is the identifying faculty, which makes a relationship between the information and the receiver. *Chitta* is a faculty of final judgment, the field of consciousness, which uses all the other three faculties.

The Self is a pure light, but the four parts of the mind are filters of different colors. When these filters are associated with the Self, the light of the Self also appears colored.

The colored filters of the mind are different forms of ignorance and that ignorance is projected onto the Self. In this way, the Self is seen acting through the mind in a state of ignorance. In fact, the light of the Self is always pure, even though it is tinted by the various colored filters of the mind. If those colored filters are removed, only one light remains, which is the light of the Self in its purest state. All duality is removed in this light. It is a state of perfect isolation, or *kaivalya*.

107

Attachment to the world is the cause of bondage; attachment to God is liberation.

TTACHMENT COMES when the senses are so attracted to an object that an alliance of object and senses is created. "World" means the desires we project onto objects, giving them a particular name and form. Simply said, our desires are our world.

When desires and objects are joined, bondage is created—a bondage of senses with the world, with our own projected desires. This creates the illusion of an alliance.

If a bird sits on a bird trapper's roller and rolls upside down, the bird grabs the roller tightly because she is afraid of falling down. The bird is free, but her fear of falling puts her in bondage, a bondage that will keep her in a cage for the rest of her life. Attachment that creates bondage is also a self-created thing. We are always free, but we are afraid of falling away from our desires. So we grab the illusion very tightly and sit in the cage of our desires for the rest of our lives.

God is truth where there is no illusion. When the mind is attached to that truth, then all bondage falls away and the self-created world of desires disappears. The mind is liberated from its bondage forever.

So the bondage of the soul is its association with matter, and its dissociation from same is liberation.

108

Non-attachment is the key that opens the doors of liberation.

OUR MIND IS ATTACHED TO THE WORLD due to our desire to live eternally. That desire creates fear of death (losing the world) and the avoidance of accepting death as a part of life. Because there is an earnest desire to live forever, so our mind colors the world according to our desires. We see the world as we want to see it: in happiness everything looks like a blooming rose, and in anger or sadness the rose looks faded, crumpled, or dried out. Due to our attachment, the reality of the world is lost and an illusory reality, based on our desires, thoughts, and emotions, appears.

When the mind develops non-attachment to objects, the objects lose their illusory form and their real form begins to appear. In this way, the more our mind gets non-attached, the more illusory appearance fades. Finally, there remains simply reality: the Self, God—or existence, consciousness, and bliss together—and that is liberation.

In order to get attached or non-attached, two are needed: the experiencer and the object. God is one, beyond attachment and non-attachment, a Supreme Consciousness.

109

*The sun's own light
is the cause of seeing the sun.
Similarly, God is seen
by God's light.*

WHEN THERE IS A COMPLETE eclipse, or when clouds are in the sky, we don't see the sun because its light is covered. To see the sun we need the sun's own light. In the same way, God is seen by God's light. God's light is higher consciousness, which is beyond words, mind, or imagination. When God's light dawns in the mind, then the mind can see God.

110

*The mind has not the reach
to know God (Brahman*);
yet God is known by a being.*

GOD, BRAHMAN, IS BEYOND mind, words, or concepts. Yet there were enlightened people who attained God and who explained the process in words as well as they could.
The mind, or *buddhi,* is the key that opens the doors of enlightenment. A person who acts selfishly in the world is using the same mind as one who works as the governor of a province, or as a saint who is living in the woods. When the mind develops ego *(ahamkara),* it becomes selfish; and when it develops dispassion, it changes to higher consciousness, or *viveka khyati*—a knowledge which discriminates Self from non-Self.

A man who was once an acrobat becomes a general in the army, and later becomes a king. In each stage, his associations reached certain levels. He could not meet a king when he was an acrobat, but when he became a general he could. As a general, he could not meet kings of other countries, but as a king he was free to do so.

In the same way, the mind in the ego *(ahamkara)* level can't discriminate between Self and non-Self, but when it attains higher consciousness it is able to discriminate. Finally, when the mind becomes its real form, the Self, it has complete reach to Brahman, or God.

So it is the same mind that acts like an ordinary person in the egoistic stage, like a saint in higher consciousness, and like an enlightened being in the state of the Self—completely free to merge into God.

---

* Formless, attributeless God.

111

Oneness is attained when the mind ceases to discriminate.

ISCRIMINATION NEEDS TWO OR MORE objects to discriminate between. When duality is wiped out, there is only one Brahman into which the aspirant dissolves.

In Yoga there are two main divisions of *samadhi*. The first is *Samprajnata Samadhi* in which there is a duality: an object and the mind. The mind concentrates on the object, progressing from its gross stage to its subtlest stage; but there is always a duality. The second and higher *samadhi* is *Asamprajnata* in which all objects, together with their support (the mind), disappear. This is a non-dual stage where there is only Brahman, which is beyond *gunas*, free from all changes, pure, without form, eternally free and one with the universal Self. Because there is nothing left to discriminate, the mind merges into Brahman (oneness).

112

*That is love
when the mind is established
in its pure form.*

THE TERM "LOVE" THAT WE USE on the worldly level is simply a mixture of attachment, expectations, feelings of pleasure, and so forth. In that kind of love, the mind switches between love and hate, pleasure and pain, attachment and aversion. Without that love, we can't function in the world. To function in the world the pairs of opposites are needed. When positivity is relatively greater, we call our state love, peace, happiness; when negativity is greater, we call it depression, pain, sadness.

Because the mind has a sense of ego, or "I am-ness," so it always relates to things which strengthen its "I am-ness." Pairs of opposites are identified as "I am this, not that" by the mind. But when the mind has no more "I am-ness," or separate existence from the Self, then a pure love shines, which is beyond the pairs of opposites. That love itself is God, or peace.

113

*Love shines naturally
when the mind stops
differentiating and separating.*

OUR MIND IS ALWAYS COMPARING things and separating them according to our wants. When the mind wants something, it gets attached to it, and if it doesn't want a thing, it creates an attitude of indifference, or labels the thing bad, ugly, undesirable. All of our judgements are based on our wanting and not wanting. In this way, we either are attached or indifferent, or jealous of things, people, and places.

There is no room for love in our heart because we are busy in our own selfishness. If the mind stops differentiating, comparing, separating according to our selfish desires, there will be no pain, pleasure, anger, or fear. The mind will dwell in a peaceful state and the heart will shine with love.

Chapter XIII
The LIBERATED ONE

114

*The universe or creation
is a question;
one who becomes its answer
is liberated.*

OUR KNOWLEDGE ABOUT THE CREATION of the universe is so minimal that it is an unanswered question. The more we try to answer this question, the more we find how little we know.

A yogi doesn't seek the answer outside, but goes within to see the Self. When one finds out about oneself one solves the question of how the universe is created, because every person is a microcosm of the macrocosm. When one becomes the answer, one is liberated from that ignorance.

115

*How can a person
who identifies with the Self
identify God with a form?*

THE SELF IS FORMLESS, BEGINNINGLESS, and immortal. The embodied Self acts as if it is the mind, senses, and the body. It appears to experience pain, pleasure, attachment, and aversion. This is wrong knowledge which is created by the union of the Self and the mind. When this wrong knowledge is removed, the Self is identified as a formless energy, and not as a body or form.

One who accepts that one is not the body cannot give a form to God, or Supreme Self. God has a form for those who have a form of their own.

116

Childhood is lost in youth;
youth is lost in old age.
One who is dead
is dead forever, except for the
one who has found God;
that person is neither
lost nor dead.

A CHILD IS BORN INNOCENT AND PURE. As the child grows, a sense of "my" and "mine" develops, and the innocence and purity of the mind start decreasing. In youth that child-like innocence and purity remain no more. A person fights for possessions, tries to compete with others, and creates his or her own world. In that world there are only two: "I am such and such," which represents that body and personality; "this is my (or mine)," which indicates a high degree of possessiveness. Vision is limited to the body and things related to the body, nothing more.

Time passes at its own rate. The person gets old, which means that the body and organs get weaker; but the desire for and attachment to that self-created world gets stronger. A fear of losing that world develops. "I may not live to enjoy my world" is the greatest fear.

For such people the body is the enjoyer and also the means of enjoyment. But the body is made up of five elements; after death the five elements separate and merge into their respective universal elements. That body is dead forever and is never reborn. For the ignorant person who identifies with the body, death is final. But one who is not lost in that ignorance identifies with the Self, or God, and never dies.

117

*The world remains
after attaining enlightenment,
but its meaning changes.*

AN ENLIGHTENED BEING FUNCTIONS in the world just as others do—eating, sleeping, showing love and sadness—but inside there is complete non-attachment to the world. For that enlightened being, the world is nothing but God. For others, the world functions with no change; they feel the same attachment, love, and hate throughout their lives.

The enlightened being, after finding peace in the Supreme Reality, experiences bliss even while experiencing the mind and the senses.

118

---

*A realized being
holds an apple in the hand
but not in the mind.*

A REALIZED BEING ACTS IN THE WORLD without attachment, selfish desires, or possessiveness. Because the mind always dwells in a state of dispassion, no action can make a print on it. If the saint holds an apple, the apple will not create a relationship of attachment, desire, or possessiveness; whereas, for an average person, all objects that are experienced with the senses will either cause attachment or repulsion. If such a person holds an apple, the mind will at once decide to whom it belongs, whether it is good or bad in taste, and so on. This is an automatic process of the mind. In an enlightened person the apple only sits in the hand and all other actions—such as, should it be eaten or put down—happen by reflex action, without any thought in the mind.

119

*To a being without desire,
the objects of the senses are
like the scattered toys
of a child tired of playing.*

OUR SENSES ARE CREATED BY THE EGO: "I am this," "I am that," "This is mine," "That is yours." The function of the senses is to establish a relationship between objects and the mind. This relationship is created by desire, which is a form of the ego of existence. As long as ego in the form of desire plays its part, we create a relationship with each object. For example, in America one needs and values a car, but one who lives in the Himalayas has no need for a car and therefore doesn't relate to a car as a valuable thing.

A child plays with toys, showing love, attachment, and possessiveness for them; but when the child gets tired of playing, he leaves the toys scattered here and there and doesn't relate to them any more. In the same way, when a person's desire is stopped, the senses don't relate to objects. To that desireless person, all objects are seen like a child's scattered toys.

120

A child and an enlightened being are both pure and happy. A child is happy in ignorance; an enlightened being is happy in knowledge.

FOR AN ENLIGHTENED BEING there is no pain because confusion is removed and the world is seen as it really is. The mind dwells in peace and happiness. All actions are selfless, innocent, and nonviolent. A child is unaware of the world. All his acts are natural and he remains happy in this thoughtless stage. There is a sameness in their purities, but a difference in their awareness.

121

*One who is
holding a lighted candle
doesn't need to be
shown the path.*

THE SELF (ATMAN) IS PURE consciousness and knowledge. It is like a lighted candle that shines by itself. It doesn't need another light to be seen; it is seen in its own light. A Self-realized person is always in that light. Like a person who is holding a lighted candle, wherever the saint goes the light goes also and the path is revealed by itself.

No one needs a light to see the sun because it is seen by its own light. In the same way, the Self is identified by its own light. Study of scriptures, Yoga, and devotion are only means to light the candle.

122

One who has learned
the lesson doesn't need
to read the books.

WE ARE BORN in a forgetful state, thinking that "I am the body." By reading scriptures, by association with spiritual people, we learn gradually that "I am the Self." One who is born with that belief, "I am the Self," has already learned the lesson and doesn't need to read scriptures.

123

*A realized being
is one whose presence creates
a feeling of peace.*

OUR ANGER, HATE, JEALOUSY, pleasure, pain, and happiness are projected from our minds all of the time. No thought that comes to the mind is limited to the mind— it creates an emotional change in the body and an emotional field around the body. For example, two people sit angry in a room and do not talk to each other. Another person who comes into the room immediately experiences that anger. If the couple sits peacefully, then any person who comes into the room will feel their peace. Similarly, if a saint has meditated in a cave for years, the mind of anyone else who sits there automatically calms down. The opposite is also true: in a cave where someone has been murdered, a person will feel disturbed.

In a realized being all thoughts are for God—there is no thought for the world. So there is always peace, and that peace permeates the surroundings. It's a natural process. Anyone who comes within that field attains peace. In that peaceful state of mind the person gets glimpses of Truth.

124

The detachment of one
who has attained illumination
is not a selfish act.

THE SENSES OF AN AVERAGE PERSON
are charmed into indulgence by sensual objects. In the presence of a non-attached being
this sense indulgence is obstructed and that
person may mistake the yogi's non-attachment for indifference.

Although indifferent to the activites of the senses,
there is no selfishness or egoism in any of the saint's actions. The senses of such a being act without desire or
attachment—seeing, hearing, touching, smelling, and eating are done by the senses as their duty.

The illumined person doesn't feel any desire for the
world and its activities. Fulfilled with the knowledge of
the Self, there is a perfect peace in that person which
soothes and creates peace in the hearts of others. The
yogi dwells in contentment—knowing that all that is to
be attained has been attained.

GLOSSARY

Ahaṁkāra: Ego; that part of the mind which identifies objects as its own and claims doership of actions.

Āgāmī Karma: Present actions which bear fruit in the future.

Ajñāna: Spiritual ignorance; the belief that the body-mind complex is the Self.

Ānanda: Bliss, see Satchidananda.

Apavarga: Liberation from the limitations of individual existence; the ultimate purpose of life.

Asamprajñāta Samādhi: Highest category of samadhi; encompasses dharma megha, "shower of virtue," and kaivalya.

Āsana: Yoga posture; third limb of Ashtanga Yoga.

Ashṭanga Yoga: Yoga system consisting of eight limbs; see Yoga.

Asmitā: The sense of pure "I-ness," "beingness," prior to emergence of ahamkara.

Asmitā Klesha: Affliction of "I-ness"; the sense of "I" as real existence and hence an obstacle to Self-realization.

Ātmān: Soul, or Self.

Ātma Sthiti: Consciousness established in Atman, or Self.

Avadhūta: An ascetic of a very high order of spiritual attainment.

Bhoga: Worldly experience, both pleasurable and painful.

Brahman: Supreme formless Reality.

Buddhi: Intellect; judgement-making function of mind.

Causal Body (Karaṇa Sharīra): First manifestation of Prakriti as individual embodiment. It reflects the qualities of the Self (absolute existence, consciousness, and bliss) and contains all the energies, functions, and faculties of the subsequent subtle and physical bodies.

Chitta: Mind stuff; basic field of consciousness which gives rise to all other mind functions; that part of mind which retains memories and samskaras in their seed forms.

Dhāraṇā: Concentration in which the mind is directed toward one object; sixth limb of Ashtanga Yoga.

Dhyāna: Meditation, deep state of concentration; seventh limb of Ashtanga Yoga.

Dispassion (Vairāgya): Realization that all forms of attachment, desire, attraction, and aversion are rooted in ignorance and are inimical to spiritual freedom.

Elements (Tattva): Five states of energy matter: ether—space, field from which other elements unfold; air—energy of movement; fire—energy of heat, radiation; water—liquid matter; earth—solid matter.

Energy Body (Sūkshma Sharīra): See Subtle Body.

Enlightenment: Stages of increased Self awareness; see Self-realization.

Guna: Component of Prakriti, the creative energy.

Guru: Spiritual preceptor; teacher.

Ichhā: Will.

Ichhā Shakti: Power inherent in Prakriti that wills to create.

Ignorance: See Ajnana.

Īshvara: God in form.

Jñāna: Knowledge; spiritual knowledge.

Jñāna Shakti: Power inherent in Prakriti that cognizes and comprehends.

Kaivalya: Perfect isolation; direct and total realization that Purusha is distinct from Prakriti; final stage of Asamprajnata Samadhi.

Karma: Action and its result. See also agami, prarabdha, and samchit karmas.

Kriyā: Method.

Kriyā Shakti: Power inherent in Prakriti that creates forms.

Liberation (Moksha): See Self-realization.

Mahābhārata: Classic Indian epic; metaphysical story about the worldly and spiritual fervor in mankind.

Mahat: Cosmic mind from which the rest of creation evolves; first evolute of Prakriti.

Manas: Faculty of mind which receives sensory data and directs the senses to act accordingly.

Māyā: Illusion; the power which makes form appear as Reality.

Mūla Prakriti: Source or root Prakriti; unmanifest Prakriti.

Nirbīja Samādhi: Samadhi without seed or mental content.

Niyama: Spiritual virtues to be cultivated; second limb of Ashtanga Yoga.

Om: Manifestation of God as sound.

Paramātman: Supreme Self; God.

Patañjali: Indian sage (300 BC) who formulated the philosophical system of Yoga.

Prakriti: The insentient creative energy of God; Nature.

Prāna: Universal life force; breath.

Prāṇāyāma: Control or expansion of prana through breath regulation; fourth limb of Ashtanga Yoga.

Prārabdha Karma: The results of past actions bearing fruit in the present.

Pratyāhāra: Introversion or collection of the outgoing tendencies of the mind; fifth limb of Ashtanga Yoga.

Puruṣa: Indwelling Reality; principle of pure, inert consciousness, active only through the creative energy of Prakriti; see Self.

Puruṣhārtha: Efforts to realize Purusha.

Rajas Guṇa: Quality of perpetual activity; a component of Prakriti.

Sādhana: Spiritual practices; efforts to achieve Yoga, or union with Self.

Saint (Sant): Seeker of Truth; Yogi; realized being.

Samadhi: Uninterrupted flow of meditation; state of super-consciousness; eighth limb of Ashtanga Yoga.

Samprajñāta Samādhi: Samadhi in which the true nature of the various levels of Prakriti is realized.

Saṁskāra: Seed imprints in the mind, the fruits of which are desires and all traits and qualities.

Sañchit Karma: Collection of karmas resulting from good, bad, and mixed actions from the past which are yet to bear fruit.

Sat: Existence; see Satchidananda.

Satchidānanda: Absolute Existence, Consciousness, and Bliss; the three qualities of God.

Sattva Guṇa: Quality of harmony, light; a component of Prakriti.

Self (Ātmā): That being which is eternal, beyond qualities, free from limitations.

Self-realization (Ātmā Jñāna): The realization of one's true nature; liberation from the limitations of the body-mind complex.

Soul (Ātmā): See Self.

Subtle Body (Sūkshma Sharīra): Non-material body which is intermediate between the causal and physical bodies; contains all the mental energies and life forces (pranas) which animate the physical body.

Tamas Guṇa: Quality of inertia, darkness; a component of Prakriti.

Tapas: Austerity; lit. "to burn," i.e. the "burning" of desires.

Viveka Khyāti, Viveka Jñāna: Discriminative knowledge or understanding; realization that the Self is distinct from the mind-body.

Yama: Spiritual restraints; the elimination of negative, self-centered tendencies which are inimical to spiritual progress; first limb of Ashtanga Yoga.

Yoga: Union of the individual with the true Self, or God; any system of spiritual practices which leads to Self-realization.

Yogi: One who practices Yoga.